Now, the authors wh
today's cults in THE DECEI
spiritual battle for people's ... ...

THE
OCCULT

In this "must-read" look at the occultic explosion in our society today, Josh McDowell and Don Stewart will guide you through a candid examination of

Astrology	Pyramid Power
Numerology	Reincarnation
Ouija Boards	Visualization & Imagery
Channeling	Satan Worship
Crystals	Demons
ESP	Witchcraft
Fire Walking	Psychic Surgery
Psychokinesis & Telekinesis	and much more . . .

THE OCCULT weighs these contemporary practices against the truth of the Scriptures and provides practical insights to help strengthen you against the satanic seductions that surround you every day. Best of all, you will discover the ultimate source of power for spiritual battle:

The Authority of the Believer Over the Powers of Darkness

*Answers to Tough Questions Skeptics Ask
About Christianity*
Josh McDowell & Don Stewart

The Dad Difference
Josh McDowell & Norm Wakefield

The Deceivers
Josh McDowell & Don Stewart

Evidence That Demands a Verdict, Volume 1
Josh McDowell

Evidence That Demands a Verdict, Volume 2
Josh McDowell

Guide to Understanding Your Bible
Josh McDowell

Handbook of Today's Religions
Josh McDowell & Don Stewart

He Walked Among Us
Josh McDowell & Bill Wilson

His Image . . . My Image
Josh McDowell

Jesus: A Biblical Defense of His Deity
Josh McDowell & Bart Larson

The Myths of Sex Education
Josh McDowell

A Ready Defense: The Best of Josh McDowell
compiled by Bill Wilson

The Resurrection Factor
Josh McDowell

*Teens Speak Out: "What I Wish My Parents Knew
About My Sexuality"*
Josh McDowell

Why Wait?
Josh McDowell & Dick Day

T H E
OCCULT

Josh McDowell
& Don Stewart

Assisted by Kurt Van Gorden

THOMAS NELSON PUBLISHERS
Nashville

First Printing, May 1992

Published by
HERE'S LIFE PUBLISHERS, INC.
P. O. Box 1576
San Bernardino, CA 92402

Cover design by David Marty Design

Library of Congress Cataloging-in-Publication Data
McDowell, Josh.
     The occult : the authority of the believer over the powers of
darkness / Josh McDowell and Don Stewart.
         p.   cm.
     Includes bibliographical references.
     ISBN 0-89840-343-X
     1. Occultism—Religious aspects—Christianity. 2. Powers
(Christian theology). I. Stewart, Don Douglas. II. Title.
BL115.O3M38   1992
261.5'1—dc20   92-9451
                                          CIP

For More Information, Write:

L.I.F.E.—P.O. Box A399, Sydney South 2000, Australia
Campus Crusade for Christ of Canada—Box 300, Vancouver, B.C., V6C 2X3, Canada
Campus Crusade for Christ—Pearl Assurance House, 4 Temple Row, Birmingham, B2 5HG, England
Lay Institute for Evangelism—P.O. Box 8786, Auckland 3, New Zealand
Campus Crusade for Christ—P.O. Box 240, Raffles City Post Office, Singapore 9117
Great Commission Movement of Nigeria—P.O. Box 500, Jos, Plateau State Nigeria, West Africa
Campus Crusade for Christ International—100 Sunport Lane, Orlando, FL 32809, U.S.A.

Contents

1

The
Occult
Phenomena

In this book we are attempting to expose the workings of Satan and the occultic realm by the standard of God's inspired Word. In doing this, it is our desire to give a balanced picture of the situation and to avoid sensationalism. Our goals include:

1. To be a source of information as to what is and what is not an occult phenomenon by clearing up certain misconceptions;

2. To keep those who are not now involved in the occult from becoming so;

3. To lead those who are now dabbling in the occult out of such practices and into a personal relationship with Jesus Christ;

4. To inform the believer who his real enemy is and the satanic devices used in spiritual warfare.

We have divided the practices of the occult into six categories. Each category has specific practices defined and analyzed. Much of the occult is refuted by a few dozen biblical passages, which are outlined in Chapter 4.

What Is the Occult?

The word *occult* comes from the Latin word *occultus* and it carries the idea of things hidden, secret and mysterious. Hoover lists three distinct characteristics of the occult:

1. The occult deals with things secret or hidden.

2. The occult deals with operations or events which seem to depend on human powers that go beyond the five senses.

3. The occult deals with the supernatural, the presence of angelic or demonic forces (David W. Hoover, *How to Respond to the Occult*, St. Louis: Concordia Publishing House, 1977, p. 8).

Under the designation *occult* we would class at least the following items: witchcraft, magic, palm reading, fortune telling, Ouija boards, tarot cards, Satanism, spiritism, demons and the use of crystal balls. To this list we could add much more.

Avoiding Extremes

C. S. Lewis commented:

There are two equal and opposite errors into which our race can fall about the devils. One is to disbelieve in their existence. The other is to believe, and to feel an unhealthy interest in them. They themselves are equally pleased by both errors and hail a materialist or magician with the same delight (C. S. Lewis, *The Screwtape Letters*, New York: MacMillan Co., 1961, preface).

It is our desire to avoid such extremes that are common in dealing with the occult. We neither see the devil in everything nor completely deny his influence and workings.

Moreover, we also intend to deal with phenomena that some feel to be occultic but can be better explained either by deception, luck, or by psychological or physiological factors.

A Word of Warning

We realize that by informing people about the world of the occult, we will be exposing certain people to things and practices of which they have previously been ignorant. It is not our desire to stimulate one's curiosity in the realm of the occult to where it becomes an obsession. Seeing that mankind has a certain fascination about evil, it would be wise to take the advice of the apostle Paul, "I want you to be wise in what is good, and innocent in what is evil" (Romans 16:19).

Playing around with the world of the occult can lead to serious repercussions, both psychologically and spiritually. There is a difference between knowing intellectually that taking poison will kill you and actually taking the poison to experience what you already knew to be a fact. We need to be aware of the workings of the satanic realm but not to the point of unhealthy fascination, obsession or involvement.

The Supernatural Does Exist

We live in a day when people are looking for answers to life's basic questions, "What is the purpose of life?"; "Is there a life after death?"; "Is there evidence for the existence of a supernatural God?"

In our other works we have given reasons why we believe that God exists and has revealed Himself to mankind through both the Bible and the Person of Jesus Christ. (See *Answers to Tough Questions, Evidence That Demands a Verdict, Vols. 1 and 2,* and *A Ready Defense.* All titles published by Here's Life Publishers.) Thus God has provided irrefutable evidence in support of the fact that He not only exists but that He is sovereign over history.

According to the Bible there is a supernatural warfare going on: "For our struggle is not against flesh and blood, but against the rulers, against the powers, against the world forces of this darkness, against the spiritual forces of wickedness in the heavenly places" (Ephesians 6:12).

This ongoing spiritual battle is between the kingdom of God and the kingdom of Satan. One purpose of Jesus Christ's coming to earth was given to us by the apostle John, "The reason the Son of God appeared was to destroy the devil's works" (1 John 3:8, NIV).

Although the Scriptures make it clear that the supernatural is real and that spiritual warfare is going on, there are those who would like to demythologize (strip the supernatural elements from) the accounts of the devil, demons and demon possession. They contend that the supernatural references in the Scriptures are from a pre-scientific, superstitious world view. However, if one takes the supernatural out of the Scriptures, all the meaning goes out with it. Dr. John Warwick Montgomery, a leading contemporary theologian, comments:

> Even the casual reader of the New Testament is aware of the pervasive recognition given to demonic powers. Again and again Jesus casts out demons, even engaging in dialogues with them (cf. the Gadarene

demoniac incident, Luke 8); and His followers cast out demons in His name (Acts 19, etc.). Jesus' public ministry commences after He is "driven by the Spirit into the wilderness to be tempted of the devil" (Matthew 4; Mark 1; Luke 4).

Central to the entire New Testament teaching concerning the end of the world is Christ's return "with all His mighty angels," God's triumph over evil powers, and the casting of Satan into the lake of fire forever (Matthew 25; Mark 13; 2 Thessalonians 1; Revelation 19, 20).

What is to be done with such material? One of my theological professors used to state flatly that the demonic in the New Testament was to be regarded as symbolic (of evil, psychosis, disease, etc.), and he became quite agitated when I asked him whether we should also regard Jesus as symbolic (of the good, of mental and physical health, etc.) since in the narrative of Jesus' temptation in the wilderness a dialogue takes place between Jesus and the devil—both evidently regarded as having comparable reality or unreality! This points up the difficulty with demythologizing of the satanic in the New Testament: They are integrally bound up with the reality of Jesus and His entire message (John Warwick Montgomery, *Principalities and Powers*, Minneapolis: Bethany Fellowship, 1973, pp. 54-55).

Those who would strip away the supernatural elements from the Scripture are left with an empty gospel, devoid of any life-transforming power. In answer to such critics, we respond with the truth and rational claims of the whole gospel—including Satan's war against it and God's supernatural intervention and ultimate triumph. The world of the occult is real, and God's all-powerful Spirit is just as real!

Occultic Deception

Although we admit the reality of the supernatural, we must be careful not to place all unexplained phenomena into the supernatural category. There is much that goes on under the guise of the supernatural that is nothing but fakery. This pseudo-occult phenomenon has fooled many people into believing in its legitimacy.

In an excellent book entitled *The Fakers,* Danny Korem and Paul Meier expose much of this phenomenon that is taken to be supernatural. They explain the difference between what is real and what is actually deception:

> What is the difference between occult and pseudo-occult phenomena? Occult phenomena are phenomena of or relating to supernatural agencies, their effects, and knowledge of them. An example which many people consider a manifestation of occultic powers is demon possession. While the manifestation is visible, the force behind it is not. We can see the *effects* of a possession, but we cannot see the demon perpetrating the manifestation. Pseudo-occult phenomena are events which *appear* to be caused by secretive, supernatural powers and yet are brought about by physical or psychological means.

> One purpose of this book is to point out the difference between the occult and pseudo-occult. There is a great danger in treating both on equal ground. One man who had purportedly performed the act of exorcism on several demon-possessed individuals tried his hand on a young teenager. The man strapped the young lady to a chair to prevent her from harming herself and proceeded with his ritual. It turned out that the girl was not demon-possessed but was schizophrenic and needed the help of a trained psychiatrist. The girl, obviously terrified by the trauma, was left in worse shape than when she first went to see the man in question.

> Misconceptions about the supernatural are legion, and it makes no difference whether one does or does not profess religious beliefs. Neither is one's level of mental competence or educational background a factor. In order for one to make qualified decisions as to whether an

event is of the supernatural or not, it is helpful if one is schooled in the art of deception (Danny Korem and Paul Meier, *The Fakers,* Grand Rapids, MI: Baker Book House, 1980, pp. 15-16).

Korem and Meier list eleven principles of deception that fakers use to imitate supernatural or occultic phenomena. These include:

1. Sleight of hand

2. Psychological principles

3. Using a stooge

4. Unseen and unknown devices

5. Mathematical principles

6. Physics

7. Physical deception

8. Mechanical deception

9. Optical illusion

10. Luck and probability

11. Combination of all the principles (ibid., pp. 22-29)

Needless to say, caution must be exercised before assuming some unexplained phenomenon is demonic. While not all Christian writers would place certain phenomena under the category of deception, as Korem and Meier, the latter clearly demonstrate the need for restraint in attributing many unexplained phenomena to the occult.

Evaluation of the Occult With the Bible, Science and Logic

Foremost in our criterion for analysis of occultic

practices is the Bible. The Bible sheds perfect light to expose the darkness of both sides of our subject. If it is pseudo-occultic, then it is a lie, and the Bible warns us about liars who intend to deceive. John 8:44 tells us the devil is a liar from the beginning and the father of lies. Revelation 22:15 says among those outside of heaven are the ones who love lies and practice them. No verse of Scripture more clearly describes the fate of those who practice lying with pseudo-occultic practices.

The other side of our biblical analysis is when a course of occultic ritual is not magician tricks, but an intervention of demonic power. This, too, the Bible answers and condemns. Those who are in league with Satan and his diabolical plan to destroy lives will be cast into the lake of eternal fire with him (Revelation 21:8).

We will use scientific analysis and logical refutation of the occult when appropriate. This is not because we view science or logic more superior than the Bible. Scripture will always be our final authority. God has granted man the gift of reason and He fully expects us to use it (Isaiah 1:18). Hard evidence and reason were appealed to a number of times in Scripture as a natural course for us to follow (Luke 1:2; John 10:38, 20:25-28; Acts 1:3, 26:25,26; 2 Peter 1:16; 1 John 1:1). When we look for hard evidence and use reason we are following the biblical model.

What Kind of People Get Involved in the Occult?

Who gets involved in the occult and why they get involved is very important. It is also important to remember that when we refer to the "occult," we do not mean one homogenous organization or religion. The "occult" refers to a collection of practices and beliefs generally associated with occultic phenomena. One

could be in the "occult" whether he is involved in a particular occultic group or just involved with occultic
practices and/or beliefs.

It is wrong to classify all occultists as either sick or
on the fringe of society, for responsible professional
people are practicing the occult. W. Elwyn Davies lists
three characteristics which may be true of occult practitioners:

1. *Many are escapists.* It has become a cliché to say
"Satan (or the demons) made me do it." The world of the
occult becomes attractive to people who find it difficult
to face up to their moral responsibilities. Many dabble
with "other powers," and are drawn into involvement.
They often claim that they have tried "other remedies" in
vain, and the alternative empowerment through the occult allures them.

2. *Many more are superstitious.* Going beyond the
bounds of revelation and common sense, they profess to
see demonic activity in many areas: Sickness, depression,
anger, any unusual or unexplained behavior. While such
may be evidence of demonic action, it should by no
means be an automatic assumption. Where natural
causes offer a reasonable explanation it is wise to accept
them as the origin of the problem. People who jump to
the conclusion that demonic influences are responsible
for a wide variety of phenomena invariably become obsessed with the thought of demons-at-work, and suffer
many of the disabilities commonly found in victims of
demonization.

3. *All are victims.* I use the word advisedly. There is
no point in being judgmental toward these people, even
though as Christians we oppose and condemn all occult
practices. From a biblical perspective there is no room for
negotiation or compromise here. God judges and condemns all traffic with demons, and we can do no less. In
the sight of God they are guilty of transgressing His law.
Each one is a victim, too—the victim of powers im-

measurably more powerful and knowing than he. What kind of person is he?

1. The curious, who experiments and plays with demonic forces, only to find eventually that they are playing with him.

2. The conformist, who looks around at this peer group and says, "Everyone does it," and decides to be another who "does it."

3. The dissatisfied, whose religious experience has left him unfulfilled and skeptical.

4. The sad, whose bereavement inclines him toward anything that offers knowledge of the dead.

5. The rebellious, who recoils from the status quo in the church and in society, and seeks a viable alternative elsewhere.

6. The psychically inclined, who wants to develop suspected latent powers.

7. The offspring of practicing occultists, who are conditioned from childhood.

8. The credulous, and every generation seems to produce its quota of them! (W. Elwyn Davies, in *Principalities and Powers*, edited by John Warwick Montgomery, Minneapolis, MN: Bethany Fellowship, 1976, pp. 303-304).

2

The
Occult
Explosion

We live in a day when occult activity is rapidly increasing. The Gallup Polls that have gained so much notoriety as a fair sampling of social trend in America provide interesting statistics about the occult from a June 1990 poll. The same questions were asked from an earlier poll (1978) and showed a rise of interest in the occult over the twelve-year span.

Based on the survey results only 7 percent deny believing in any of the eighteen paranormal phenomena. Belief in the devil rose from 39 percent in 1978 to 55 percent in 1990. *Déjà vu* was formerly the experience of 30 percent of those polled. It rose to 55 percent in the recent study. Clairvoyance had a slight increase of 2 percent, while ESP decreased by the same. Astrology was off by 4 percent in the new poll, but belief in ghosts jumped from 11 percent in 1978 to 25 percent in 1990, and belief in witches climbed from 10 percent to 14 percent.

In addition, the late Dr. Walter R. Martin, the leading expert on cults and the occult in America, said that 60 million Americans dabble in the New Age or occultic practices. Where occult bookstores were taboo in earlier decades, the market exploded to accommodate 2,500 New Age and occult bookstores by 1988 (cf., *The New Cults*, Minneapolis: Bethany House Publishers, 1989, pp. 7-8). There are more than 3,000 publishers of occult books and magazines with a combined revenue of one-billion dollars in annual sales. Shirley MacLaine sponsors seminars that raised 3 million dollars between 1989 and 1990 to build her New Age Center near Baca, Colorado (ibid., p. 21).

Martin Ebon, former administrative secretary of the Parapsychology Foundation, and the author of *The Satan Trap* and *Dangers of the Occult*, gives his assessment of the upswing of interest in occult phenomena:

> Occult practices and psychic phenomena are exercising a hold on millions of Americans today. There is no single explanation for this boom, but its major causes are easy to pinpoint. To begin with, the age-old pull of the irrational remains as persistent and just about as inexplicable as, let's say, terrestrial gravity; and while traditional religious practices lose their attraction, the occult and related Eastern mysticism gain in popularity.
>
> Two mass stimuli have contributed to this trend. One is the drug cult, which causes an interest in such matters as a "non-drug high," to be sought in meditation and similar practices, as well as in confirmation of the drug-induced feeling that mind may control matter or events. Second, a series of highly popular motion pictures created successive waves of occult or pseudo-occult involvements. With *Rosemary's Baby*, which pictured the birth of a diabolical infant, came an upswing in witchcraft practices; with *The Exorcist*, demonic possession and exorcism were dramatized to a public of

millions; other films and television shows have dealt with similar themes.

These waves of interest, compounded, have indirectly drawn attention to scholarly research of parapsychology—although researchers in the field deplore the sensationalism that powers public interest. The mass-circulation tabloids, in particular the *National Enquirer*, bring a weekly potion of the magical and psychic to the check-out counters of the nation's supermarkets; stories of miraculous healings, haunted houses, visits by Unidentified Flying Objects, and exorcism abound in these periodicals. The very fact that these shrewdly edited publications find it profitable to mix the occult with jet-set gossip and anecdotes of awe and uplift illustrates public fascination with psychic subjects. Astrology, although in a category by itself, has a similar hold on a large public ("The Occult Temptation," *The Humanist*, January/February 1977).

From the above it is evident that occult beliefs have now penetrated every web of our society. From the media to grocery stores, one cannot turn without encountering some type of occultic literature or influence. One can find horoscopes for weight loss and horoscopes for a better sex life.

Even higher education is not exempt. The University of California at Berkeley and other institutions of higher education offer courses in magic, witchcraft and parapsychology.

Parapsychology is an attempt to give certain occultic practices scientific respectability. This often means assenting to their reality (such as mental telepathy, telekinesis) yet having no explanation for their source, or the means by which they operate.

Why Is There Such an Interest in the Occult?

With the alarming rate at which people are becoming involved in the occult, the inevitable question of

"why" comes up. Why do people who live in this enlightened age with all the marvelous scientific and
technological advances become involved in occultic
practices? We believe there are several factors that have
contributed to the rise of occult popularity.

The Secularization of the Gospel

In recent years there has been a denial of the cardinal doctrines of the Christian faith from those
occupying a position of leadership in the church. This
leaves a greater spiritual vacuum in the world, which
invites people who have spiritual needs to go elsewhere
to have them satisfied. Moreover, some of these church
leaders who have forsaken the gospel have themselves
become practitioners of the occult, causing a follow-the-
leader mentality in many former churchgoers.

The classic example would be the late Episcopal
bishop, James Pike, who rejected the church's belief in
the deity of Christ, His virgin birth, and other central
truths. After the suicide death of his son, Pike began to
consult mediums, including the famous Arthur Ford, in
an attempt to contact the spirit of his dead son. Pike became a firm believer in life after death from his occultic
involvement rather than from biblical doctrine and took
many people with him to the dark world of the occult.
When the church "waters down" the gospel of Christ,
the door to occultic practice swings wide open.

Curiosity

There is a certain mystery about the occult which
appeals to our curiosity. Many who get involved in occult practices do so by starting out with so-called
"harmless" practices such as reading horoscopes or
using a Ouija board. They afterward proceed into
deeper involvement because of an increasing curiosity.
Buzzard comments upon this fascination:

Our age seems to have a deep fascination with evil, the bizarre, and the inexplicable. It thrives on horror and repulsion. What makes one faint or vomit or experience nightmares has a kind of magnetic charm. Mary Knoblauch summed up this fascination in commenting on *The Exorcist:* "Perhaps the most frightening thing about *The Exorcist* is that thirst for and fascination with evil that lies buried in us all, surfacing with savage swiftness at the right incarnation." The moment of that incarnation seems to be upon us. What was buried has arisen and dances unashamedly in the streets (Lynn Buzzard, *Demon Possession,* edited by John Warwick Montgomery, Minneapolis: Bethany Fellowship, 1976, Introduction, pp. 17-18).

Unfortunately, there is a price to pay for this curiosity about the occult. The occult is not something neutral that an individual can get in and out of without any adverse effects.

In his book *Kingdom of Darkness,* F. W. Thomas relates a story of a man-and-wife journalistic team who desired to investigate the occult in London. They joined a satanic group to obtain firsthand information, but eventually withdrew because of the frightening things which they observed. Their lives were never the same. They were troubled by many terrible experiences and incidents.

Thomas concluded, "Such was the experience of an unwise couple whose curiosity for black magic dragged them through untold anguish and despair. One cannot just pick up the dark bolts of magical fire and drop them at will without getting burned. There is always a price to pay for use of these forbidden powers, in this world as well as in the world to come" (cited by Clifford Wilson and John Weldon, *Occult Shock and Psychic Forces,* San Diego: Master Books, 1980, pp. 13-14).

The Occult Offers Reality

There is a reality in the occultic experience which attracts many people to it. All of us desire some sort of ultimate answer for life's basic questions, and the world of the occult gladly supplies the answers. The astrologist will chart your future. The Ouija board promises you direction, and the medium talking to the spirit of your dead relative informs you that things are fine in the next world.

Since these occultic practices do reveal some amazing things, the practitioner is lulled into thinking that he has experienced ultimate reality and no longer needs to continue his search for truth. The spiritual vacuum is filled by means of a spiritual experience, not with God, but often from the very pit of hell.

A Sign of the Times

There are many indications that we are living at the end of the age with the return of Jesus Christ on the horizon. If this is the case, then we should expect to see an increase in demonic activity as Christ's coming nears, for this is the clear teaching of Scripture: "But the Spirit explicitly says that in later times some will fall away from the faith, paying attention to deceitful spirits and doctrines of demons" (1 Timothy 4:1).

Jesus said that at the end of the age, "false Christs and false prophets will arise, and will show signs and wonders, in order, if possible, to lead the elect astray" (Mark 13:22). Thus, Scripture indicates that occultic activity would be on the rise shortly before the second coming of Jesus Christ.

3

How
the
Occult
Is Promoted

Ŋone of us are immune to the effects of our environment upon our thoughts and conduct. Our minds are always filtering incoming data. Whether it is in the form of advertising, television, movies, music, magazines, newspapers, books, conversations, speeches, sermons, or any other source, we are in the continual process of discarding what we think is bad and keeping what we think is good. Your thoughts, in fact, are what you use for analysis of the information.

If someone could persuade you to think differently, then you would accept the things that would normally be discarded. Christians, especially, have been the target of secular humanists and other antagonists who call us "intolerant, narrow-minded, religious bigots," and other names, to break down our defenses and try to stop us from holding values of a biblical nature.

Their devious plan has worked on some Christians. How often have you been surprised to find that a Christian you respected has changed his view on a major issue? Very seldom has the name-calling humanist stopped to realize that he cannot call you intolerant unless he is also intolerant of your beliefs. He cannot call the Christian way bigoted unless he is also bigoted against Christianity. He cannot call us narrow-mined unless he is also narrow-minded against us.

Is it important or even necessary to guard our hearts and minds from the persuasion of the world? Yes, it is. What some people considered unthinkable at previous times in their life is what they so often bend toward in their moments of weakness. Jesus gave us some guidelines for protection in the Sermon on the Mount. "The lamp of the body is the eye," He said. "If therefore your eye is clear, your whole body will be full of light. But if your eye is bad, your whole body will be full of darkness. If therefore the light that is in you is darkness, how great is the darkness!" (Matthew 6:22,23) We are in whole-hearted agreement with Jesus. We believe that our behavior needs to be guarded by the light of God's Word, which also means we need to be careful about what we allow to enter our body through our senses—especially the eyes and ears.

Those who have been raised to attend church or perhaps have helped teach children's church programs will probably be familiar with the children's song, "Be careful, little eyes, what you see ... be careful, little ears, what you hear ... " Sometimes the most profound truths arise from the simplest examples. Teenagers and adults should sing that song as loudly as the children do because we are exposed to more things than the children.

Stephen P. Lawhead speaks boldly to adults in his book *Turn Back the Night* (Worchester, IL: Crossway Books, 1985), telling us how we need to stop giving in to the media ploys that are shaping our culture. The four major mediums—books, music, television and movies—cannot be underestimated for their powerful persuasion. The relaxed censorship of the FCC has provided a venue of anarchy over the television waves. God is blasphemed, Christianity is ridiculed, preachers are seen as charlatans, fornication is the norm, homosexuality is permissive, drugs are for parties, and all of this is done in the name of constitutional freedom.

The stage has been set for indoctrinating adults on New Age trends and teenagers on the occult and satanism. Television, movies, books and music have become the pulpit for the occult. Their preachers are the movie stars and the rock stars. And the converts are persuaded to embrace the doctrines of the occult with an openness that would make advertisers jealous. Open-mindedness is what they call it, but we would like to give a word of caution ascribed to an Episcopal bishop, "It's a fine thing to have an open mind, but not so open so as your brains fall out."

The Occult in Printed Media

Practically every daily newspaper in the country is a source for horoscopes. Some people read them for amusement, some out of curiosity. Eventually belief sets in and it becomes a regular part of daily guidance. Teenage magazines contain horoscopes and heavy metal magazines offer a variety of occultic paraphernalia through mail-order. Heavy metal albums and CDs boldly picture satanic symbols in support of the band's world view. Novels are published for teenagers and adults with themes involving satanic ritual (often inaccurate) and occult mysticism.

These novels capture the vivid imagination of the readers, stimulating new interest in the works of Satan. They frequently forget that they are engrossed in fiction and take as reality the illusionary theme. The gate of the mind is opening wider for the reader of occult novels and satanism.

Younger children are not exempt from the onslaught of perversion. Comic books containing the subject of the occult are too profitable for the publishers to tone it down. Christian researchers Bob and Gretchen Passantino show the link between satanic themes and comics in their book *When the Devil Dares Your Kids*:

> Comic books provide teenagers with exciting stories and larger-than-life role models. Unfortunately, many of the new comics, some labeled 'for mature readers,' also provide readers with graphic images of infidelity, sexual perversion, including necrophilia and oral sex, black magic, destructive occultism, rape, murder, mutilation, homosexuality, sado-masochism, and foul language (Ann Arbor, MI: Servant Books, 1991, p. 128).

We would have to include games under the subject of printed media. Some of the most esoteric ideas associated with magic and occult ritual, which would take the average researcher years to compile, are now neatly packaged in games for teenagers. The fantasy role-playing game *Dungeons and Dragons* is one case in point. Those who believe it is a harmless game for expanding the imagination have not read the accounts of suicide and crime carried out by its participants. A sampling of direct quotations from the *Dungeon Master's Guide* reveals the prevalence of Satanism:

> Whether or not the character actively professes some deity, he or she will have an alignment and serve one or more deities of this general alignment indirectly or unbeknownst to the character (p. 25).

> The spell caster should be required to show you what form of protective inscription he or she has used when the spell is cast. According to experts in witchcraft

and satanic worship the three forms mentioned are: Pictures of a magic circle, pentagram, and thaumaturgic triangle (p. 42).

"Elric (hero)"—the sign being given by his left hand (which is called the Goat Head sign) means "Satan is lord" to all Satan worshipers (p. 86). Joan Hake Robie has done an excellent job documenting the occultic and satanic nature of *Dungeons and Dragons* (cf., *The Truth About Dungeons and Dragons*, Lancaster, PA: Starburst Publishers, 1991).

The Occult in Music

Eric Holmberg's nonsensational research into rock and roll music reveals a trend of Satanism and occultism on album covers and in lyrics since the 1960s. Mr. Holmberg gives a revealing look at how Christianity is mocked and the occult is exalted in his video presentation *Hell's Bells* (Gainsville, FL: Reel to Real Ministries, 1989). Mr. Holmberg points out:

> Jesus has become the focus of more ridicule in rock and roll than any other personality. Every facet of his life and mission is criticized and mocked ... Jefferson Airplane's song *The Son of Jesus* is filled with sacrilege, suggesting that, among other things, Jesus was involved in the occult, had bastard children through Mary Magdalene ... Groups like LudiChrist, Coven, Dark Wizard and virtually dozens of other groups openly sing about wickedness that, until recently, could not be found outside occult book stores.
>
> There is no symbol of satanism more bold than the pentagram, the downward pointing star with the goat's head. Next the inverted cross (to desecrate and mock the crucifixion), there is no symbol more common to the rock and roll industry than the pentagram. Motley Crue, Slayer, Be Bop Deluxe, Metal Fatigue, Venom, Sam Kinison, Suicidal Tendencies, The Plasmatics, and

AC/DC are among just a few groups where the satanic symbol is used.

The satanic hand sign with the index finger and little finger extended from a closed hand is seen at nearly every rock concert and on album covers since the days of the Beatles's *Yellow Submarine* album. Holmberg says, "The vast majority of concert goers have no idea what the symbol means when they flash the sign at a concert" (ibid.).

The rock and roll industry has pushed Satanism and the occult to the forefront as merchandise for teenagers and youngsters. Holmberg points out how hard-rock and heavy-metal bands openly desire hell and make it the theme of many songs, as these titles reveal, *Go To Hell* (Alice Cooper), *Hotter Than Hell* (Kiss), *Aloha From Hell* (Cramps), *See You in Hell* (Grim Reaper), *Citizens of Hell* (CJSS), *Condemned to Hell* (Rigor Mortis), *Highway to Hell* (AC/DC), *Burn in Hell* (Twisted Sister), *Gonna Raise Hell* (Chevy Truck), *Princess of Hell* (Merciful Fate) and *Hell Patrol* (Raven). The parents of today have pushed their children behind closed doors to listen to their music which then becomes an unsupervised indoctrination right in the household.

Rap music has more sexually explicit terms and less overt Satanism, but it is nonetheless present in a few groups. A good evaluation of the occult in rap music is Eric Holmberg's *All Wrapped Up* (Reel to Real Ministries, 1991).

The Occult in Television

This twentieth-century marvel brings Satanism and the occult into more homes in America than any other source. Children, who are too young for heavy-metal bands, receive a heavy dose of the occult through their favorite "hero" cartoons. A full 98 percent of

American homes have at least one television set and 60 percent have two or more. Fifty-three percent have video cassette recorders. Television is a teaching tool as well as an entertainment center. The problem is what we allow it to teach.

Preschool children (ages two to five) watch an average of twenty-eight hours of television weekly. Trailing close behind are their older brothers and sisters (ages six to eleven) who manage to watch 23.5 hours of television each week with fewer hours spent in the home! A preschooler will spend more hours before the television than it will take him to earn a college degree. By the time he completes high school, the average American child will log 22,000 hours of television.

The potential danger of secular humanism and utter garbage that is impressed upon the memory banks of American youth through television cannot be stressed enough. The problem becomes colossal and shocks most parents when they find that Eastern philosophy, the occult, and satanic teachings are commonplace in Saturday morning animation. Monism (all is one), pantheism (all is god), shamans, wizards, magicians, witches, covens, ancient occult books, demon possession, and exorcism provide a short list of the teachings presented. The electronic baby sitter is not a baby sitter at all, it is an electronic teacher with scripts written by those who have everything but a Christian world view.

Author Phil Phillips painstakingly documents the number of violent acts done in cartoons during any given Saturday morning. Although he draws conclusions from his research that we may not entirely agree with, his premise is correct. We cannot ignore that the funny little characters and the super-dynamic heros of Saturday morning are teaching children incorrect ways to think about life (cf., *Saturday Morning Mind Control*, Nashville: Oliver Nelson, 1991).

If the theme of Satanism and the occult runs deep into heavy-metal music, then it is not a surprise that music videos have become a promotional tool in Satan's toolbox. Watch any segment of MTV or a secular rock concert on television and you will witness the occultic overtone of the rock and roll generation. At concerts, 20,000 hands pound the air in rhythm to the music flashing the "horn" of the "Devil's sign." The satanic lyrics are not changed for MTV. Whether it is Alice Cooper or the occultism of AC/DC, each super-star of the platinum record has his time-slot on MTV.

The television is a box that transmits what the receiver is tuned to. It has no knowledge, morals or feelings, and only shows what its owner permits. It can be used to bring corruption into the home or it can be used to bring wholesome programming and Christian programs into the home. The choice is up to its owner.

The Occult in Movies

A host of horror and gore films not able to be edited for television have hit the theaters every year and are on the top ten list at video stores. A scary film used to be *King Kong* or *Godzilla*, but those years are far gone and replaced with life-like visual effects of satanic ritual. The macabre of the past never glorified the occult as today's films do.

Bob and Gretchen Passantino relate how the occult has become a staple in the movie industry:

> Movies and Satan? Most parents remember *Rosemary's Baby*, *The Exorcist*, and *Damien*. Most would probably add to the group the shock-schlock of the *Halloween* and *Nightmare on Elm Street* series. Of course we can throw in the B-movie horror flicks shown on local stations on sleepy Saturday nights.

But the movie invasion of the occult goes far beyond these slick presentations. More than two hundred horror movies from the mainline producers and distributors littered the theater landscape between 1980 and 1990 . . . many took occult powers for granted and seriously presented a world view of occult victimization (op. cit., p. 120).

Let us return to our opening remarks. Be careful, little eyes, what you see. Be careful, little ears, what you hear. How easy it is to ignore what we have taught youngsters. We must remember what the apostle John wrote about our relationship to the world:

Do not love the world, nor the things in the world. If any one loves the world, the love of the Father is not in him. For all that is in the world, the lust of the flesh and the lust of the eyes and the boastful pride of life, is not from the Father, but is from the world (1 John 2:15,16).

4

What
the
Bible Says
About the
Occult

T he Bible categorically denounces any and all occultic practices:

When you enter the land which the LORD your God
gives you, you shall not learn to imitate the detestable
things of those nations.

There shall not be found among you anyone who
makes his son or his daughter pass through the fire, one
who uses divination, one who practices witchcraft, or
one who interprets omens, or a sorcerer, or one who casts
a spell, or a medium, or a spiritualist, or one who calls up
the dead.

For whoever does these things is detestable to the
LORD; and because of these detestable things the LORD
your God will drive them out before you.

You shall be blameless before the LORD your God.

For those nations, which you shall dispossess, listen
to those who practice witchcraft and to diviners, but as

for you, the Lord your God has not allowed you to do so
(Deuteronomy 18:9-14).

In the same manner, the New Testament condemns such workings (Galatians 5:20). In the city of
Ephesus many who were practicing in the occult became believers in Jesus Christ and renounced their
occultic practices: "And many of those who practiced
magic brought their books together and began burning
them in the sight of all" (Acts 19:19).

Another encounter with the occult can be seen in
Acts 13:6-12:

> And when they had gone through the whole island
> as far as Paphos, they found a certain magician, a Jewish
> false prophet whose name was Bar-Jesus, who was with
> the proconsul, Sergius Paulus, a man of intelligence. This
> man summoned Barnabas and Saul and sought to hear
> the word of God.
>
> But Elymas the magician (for thus his name is trans-
> lated) was opposing them, seeking to turn the proconsul
> away from the faith.
>
> But Saul, who was also known as Paul, filled with
> the Holy Spirit, fixed his gaze upon him, and said, "You
> who are full of all deceit and fraud, you son of the devil,
> you enemy of all righteousness, will you not cease to
> make crooked the straight ways of the Lord?
>
> "And now, behold, the hand of the Lord is upon you,
> and you will be blind and not see the sun for a time."
> And immediately a mist and a darkness fell upon him,
> and he went about seeking those who would lead him by
> the hand.
>
> Then the proconsul believed when he saw what had
> happened, being amazed at the teaching of the Lord.

The false prophet who called himself Bar-Jesus
(Son of Jesus) was actually trying to keep the governor,
Sergius Paulus, from becoming a believer, and the judg-

ment of blindness on this man was immediate. Walter Martin makes some astute observations on the passage by listing five characteristics of those who oppose God:

1. They are in league with Satan and possess certain supernatural powers.

2. They are false prophets.

3. They seek to influence people politically and ecclesiastically, particularly those in positions of power (verses 6,7).

4. They attempt to prevent those who are seeking to hear the Word of God from learning it by opposing those who preach it (verse 8).

5. They deliberately attempt to divert prospective converts from the faith (verse 8) as their ultimate goal (Walter Martin, *The Maze of Mormonism*, Santa Ana, CA: Vision House Publishers, Inc., 1977, pp. 216-17).

From the above, to which much could be added, we see how the Bible in the strongest terms condemns the occult and those who practice it. The road of the occult is broad and leads to destruction, while the way of Christ is narrow and leads to life eternal.

We will devote lengthy discussions to the nature of Satan and demons in later chapters. The manner in which they deceive the human race is our present study. They use a number of means specifically mentioned in Scripture, including, but not limited to, astrology, divination (fortune-telling), enchantments (incantations), magic, mediumship, omens, prognostication (soothsayer, clairvoyance), sorcery, spiritism (necromancy), witchcraft, and wizardry (channeling).

Astrology is sometimes referred to as "observing times" in the Old Testament (Deuteronomy 18:10, KJV).

It includes the practice of horoscopes and predictions by the planets. God rebukes Israel for placing any stock in this practice (Isaiah 47:12,13).

When Daniel, a prophet of God, was compared to the Babylonian astrologers, it was said that he knew ten times more than they did (Daniel 1:20). The astrologers of Daniel's time were not able to interpret King Nebuchadnezzar's dream (Daniel 2:11), so he decreed that they should be killed (Daniel 2:13). Daniel succeeded where the astrologers failed, because he sought God (Daniel 2:18,19). The showdown between the Babylonian astrologers and Daniel occurred again in Daniel 5:7-16. God gave Daniel the interpretation of the handwriting on the wall for King Belshazzar (Daniel 5:17), which again showed the failure of the astrologers.

Divination is an act of fortune-telling. This practice is condemned by several prophets in the Bible (Deuteronomy 18:9-14; Isaiah 44:25; Jeremiah 27:9).

The Lord calls the word of the diviners a lie (Ezekiel 13:8) and cuts them off from cohabitation with Israel (Ezekiel 13:9). The law of Moses made it punishable by death (Leviticus 20:27), but its existence always filtered into Israel through the pagan cultures around them (Ezekiel 21:21). Jeremiah calls divination a deception (14:14), and Isaiah says God will make them into fools (44:25).

In the New Testament times, divining was a lucrative business at Philippi (Acts 16:16). Paul took authority over the demon that inspired the girl's practice and cast it out (16:18), which shows us that not all divination is educated guesswork, but may be a result of demonic influence.

Enchantments are referred to as incantations by some Bible translators. In the showdown between Moses and the wizards, enchanters and those with magic books (Exodus 7:11), they were no match for what God did through Moses. They could only imitate the genuine that Moses did, but after the first three miracles of Moses, they gave up and acknowledged that God was working through Moses (8:19). Sometimes enchantments are called spells or charming in the Bible, and are condemned by God (Deuteronomy 18:10-12, KJV; Isaiah 19:3, KJV).

Magic is another source of occultism forbidden by God. Although most magicians today will readily admit theirs is explainable by sleight-of-hand, misdirection, and other illusions, some intentionally deceive the gullible and pretend to have supernatural power over elements. In the example of Moses before Pharaoh, there were three classes of men who tried to withstand him—the wise men, enchanters and those with magic books (Exodus 7:11). So obvious was their inferiority to the real miracles of Moses that Aaron's rod, once it was a snake, swallowed up their snakes, which were probably produced by sleight-of-hand (7:12).

For us to think that Moses, or any other prophet, was at any moment deceived by the trickery of the magicians is to ignore what Paul said to Bar-Jesus in Acts 13:6-12. Here, Paul points out the essence of the magician's power, "You are full of deceit and fraud . . . " Paul knew that the man deceived the people by claiming powers that were not his.

Sometimes the act of self-deception enters in. There are some magicians today who promote themselves as having supernatural power, which is self-deception. Perhaps some of those in biblical times, like Bar-Jesus, had deceived themselves before they had deceived the people. God condemns it either way, saying it is akin to enchantments, spells and sorcery (Deuteronomy 18:10-12).

Mediumship, otherwise called spiritism or necromancy, is the attempt at conjuring up the dead through seances or a medium. This is strictly forbidden by God (Deuteronomy 18:10-12). It is distinguished from wizardry, which usually has a familiar spirit, much similar to channeling in the New Age (cf., *Tyndale Old Testament Commentary, Deuteronomy*, p. 211).

The practice of mediumship is also forbidden in 2 Kings 21:6. A medium's presence in Israel is called a defilement in Leviticus 19:31. Isaiah said we are not to seek the dead on behalf of the living, and the mediums have no light in them (8:19,20).

Omens or signs are not to be sought out for direction in life. The Lord rebuked Israel for seeking after omens. He caused the omens to fail just so they would see their folly (Isaiah 44:25). He tells us in Deuteronomy 18:10-12 it is an abomination to seek omens.

Prognostication, soothsaying, and clairvoyance are the practice of having innate knowledge of the future. The prognosticators were proven to be liars and faulty in their predictions. They had no power to save Israel (Isaiah 47:13-15). Jeremiah says they predict lies that can only bring forth expulsion and death (27:9,10). They were utter failures in knowing Nebuchadnezzar's dream (Daniel 2:27). God forbids them to associate with Israel, saying they are an abomination (Deuteronomy 18:10-12).

Sorcery, or the practice of cutting herbs, as the literal Hebrew has it, is the possible use of drugs. This was practiced by Egyptians (Exodus 7:11) and the Babylonians (Isaiah 47:9-15), but is forbidden by God in both the Old Testament and the New Testament (Deuteronomy 18:10-12; Micah 5:12; Galatians 5:20; Revelation 21:8). In the New Testament, Philip confronted Simon, who was a sorcerer in Samaria. Simon thought he could purchase the power of God and offered money for the Holy Spirit, which drew a sharp rebuke from Peter (Acts 8:9-24). In another case, Paul was in Ephesis, where sorcery was widely practiced. After conversion of several prominent people, they gathered the books on sorcery together and burned them (Acts 19:19).

Witchcraft is the dualistic practice of worshiping the god and goddess of nature. Often it is mixed with sorcery and other occultism, including rituals for gaining power over elements. It is forbidden by God in Deuteronomy 18:10-12 and Micah 5:12. Peace was removed from the land because Jezebel practiced witchcraft (2 Kings 9:22). King Saul disobeyed God and sought after the witch of En Dor, who apparently practiced spiritism. As a result, it cost him his life (1 Samuel 28). Witchcraft is condemned in the New Testament through Paul's letter to Galatia (5:20).

A wizard is one who has a familiar spirit. A familiar spirit in the Old Testament was a spirit that had regular contact with the wizard. This is the same as what New Agers practice when they claim to have a spirit-guide or channel for a spirit. The spirits often speak through them (automatic speaking) or write through them (automatic writing). Wizardry is forbidden by God (Deuteronomy 18:10-12), and those who practice it have no truth in them (Isaiah 8:20).

5

Divination

and

Fortune-telling

Divination, the art of forecasting the future supposedly by supernatural means, is an ancient practice which is still popular today. Divination is also known as fortune-telling. The one who practices this activity is know as a diviner. The diviner makes use of various props to receive his knowledge, including palmistry, cartomancy, mirror gazing and psychometry. Some knowledge may come by means of contact with demonic beings, and some is merely educated guesses and trickery. An example in the Bible where there was a demonic spirit in control of the diviner is found in Acts 16:16.

There are those who see fortune-telling as a con game without any supernatural phenomena occurring. The fortune-teller, rather than making contact with the spirit world, is a con artist duping the unsuspecting victims. Danny Korem lists certain techniques used by fortune-tellers which give realism to their readings:

1. Observation of sensory clues.

2. Prior knowledge of subject obtained secretly before reading.

3. Ability to think on one's feet and change direction of the reading without hesitation or detection.

4. Understanding of human nature.

5. Utilization of the cards or any other apparatus to pick up sensory clues or change the direction of the reading when off the track.

6. An element of luck and a keen sense of playing the odds so that a well-placed guess may produce spectacular results (Danny Korem and Paul Meier, *The Fakers*, Grand Rapids, MI: Baker Book House, 1980, p. 107).

Whether all fortune-telling is nothing but a glorified con game remains a matter of debate. What is not debatable is the fact that any and all types of attempting to divine the future through fortunetelling is an abomination to God. God has already revealed to us in His Word the basic program for the future, and He condemns in the strongest of terms those who would try to find out what is going to occur without consulting Him. The person, instead of looking to God for direction, is in disobedience by seeking fortune-tellers to receive guidance for his life.

Satan has accomplished his purpose, which is getting people away from worshiping the true and living God. Since fortune-telling does this, it should never be practiced even for fun. It is a device of the devil which takes one further away from the Kingdom of God. First Chronicles 10:13,14 records God's punishment on Saul for going to a medium instead of God:

> So Saul died for his trespass which he committed against the LORD, because of the word of the LORD which

he did not keep; and also because he asked counsel of a medium, making inquiry of it, and did not inquire of the LORD. Therefore He killed him, and turned the kingdom to David the son of Jesse.

Some would put fortune-telling in the area of the divine, insisting God had given the fortune-tellers their ability. However, this could not be the case since Scripture condemns such practices.

Astrology

Astrology is an ancient practice that assumes that the position of the stars and planets has a direct influence upon people and events. Supposedly, one's life pattern can be charted by determining the position of the stars and planets at the time of one's birth. The chart that attempts to accomplish this is known as a "horoscope." Rene Noorbergen explains how one's horoscope is charted:

> For every personal horoscope, the moment of birth is the essential starting point. This, coupled with the latitude and longitude of the individual's birthplace, provides the initial package for the usual astrological chart. While this is elementary, it is not complete; a factor known as "true local time" must also be considered. This "true" time is arrived at by adding or subtracting four minutes for each degree of longitude that your birthplace lies to the east or west of the center of your time zone of birth. Once this has been accomplished, the next step is to convert this "true" time into "sidereal" or star time. This is done with the aid of an ephemerus, a reference book showing the positions of the planets in relationship to the earth. Checking this star time in an astrological table is the last formal move, for in doing so, the theme of the individual's "ascendant"—the astrological sign that is supposed to have been rising on the eastern horizon at the moment of birth—is revealed.

Once you have developed this data—these simple

steps are no more difficult than solving a seventh-grade math problem—then you are ready to "chart" your horoscope. This means you align the "ascendant" with the nine-o'clock point on the inner circle of the horoscope, and from there you are prepared to "read" the various zodiacal "houses" that control your life and fortune (Rene Noorbergen, *The Soul Hustlers*, Grand Rapids, MI: Zondervan, 1976, pp. 176-177).

How Is It Justified?

How astrologers justify their practice is explained by Michael Van Buskirk:

One's future can be forecast, allegedly, because astrology asserts the unity of all things. This is the belief that the Whole (or all of the universe put together) is in some way the same as the Part (or the individual component or man), or that the Part is a smaller reflection of the Whole (macrocosmic/microcosmic model). The position of the planets (the macro) influences and produces a corresponding reaction in man (the micro). This makes man a pawn in the cosmos with his life and actions predetermined and unalterable (Michael Van Buskirk, *Astrology: Revival in the Cosmic Garden*, Costa Mesa, CA: Answers in Action, 1976, p. 6).

Noorbergen concludes, "To believe in astrology, you must support the philosophy that you are either a 'born loser' or a 'born winner.' The stars, we are being told, do not merely forecast the curse of our lives, but they also cause the events to take place. They both impel and compel" (Rene Noorbergen, op. cit., pp. 178-179).

The Problems of Astrology

The claims that astrologists have made have drawn several criticisms from the scientific community. In September, 1975, 186 prominent American scientists, along with eighteen Nobel Prize winners, spoke out against "the pretentious claims of astrological char-latans," saying, among other things, that there is no scientific basis whatsoever for the assumption that the stars foretell events and influence lives. The following are some of the reasons the practice of astrology must be rejected as both unscientific and unbiblical.

The Problem of Authority

Astrologists are victims of their own system. They cannot have the objective authority necessary to explain our own world. If everything is predetermined in conjunction with the zodiac, then how can the astrologists get outside of that fatalism to accurately observe it?

What if the astrologists themselves are predetermined to explain everything by astrology? There is no way they can prove their system if they are pawns in that same system. By contrast, as Christians we can test our own world view because someone, Jesus Christ, has come from outside the "system" to tell us, objectively, what our system is like.

Conflicting Systems

The problem of authority in astrology is graphically revealed when one realizes there are many systems of astrology which are diametrically opposed to each other. Astrologers in the West would not interpret a horoscope the same way a Chinese astrologer would.

Even in the West, there is no unanimity of interpretation among astrologers, seeing that some contend for eight zodiac signs rather than twelve, while others argue for fourteen or even twenty-four signs of the zodiac.

With these different systems employed by astrologers, an individual may go to two different astrologers and receive two totally opposed courses of behavior for the same day! This is not only a possibility, it is also a reality, for a simple comparison between astrological forecasts in daily newspapers will often reveal contradictions.

Earth-Centered Viewpoint

Astrology is based upon the premise that the planets revolve around the earth, known as the "geocentric theory." This theory was shown to be in error by Copernicus, who proved that the planets revolve around the sun, not the earth. This is known as the "heliocentric theory."

Since astrology is based upon the refuted geocentric theory, its reliability is destroyed. Since the basic assumption is false, all conclusions, even if feebly reinterpreted by today's knowledge and drawn from this assumption, are likewise false.

Missing Planets

One of the major misconceptions that is the basis of astrology concerns the number of planets in our solar system. Most astrological charts are based upon the assumption that there are seven planets in our solar system (including the sun and the moon).

In ancient times, Uranus, Neptune and Pluto were unobservable with the naked eye. Consequently, astrologers based their system upon the seven planets they believed revolved around the earth. Since that time, it has been proven that the sun, not the earth, is the center of the solar system and that three other planets exist in our solar system.

According to the astrological theory that the position of the planets has a definite influence upon human behavior and events, these three previously undiscovered planets should also have an influence upon behavior and must be considered to cast an exact horoscope. Since they usually are not considered, the astrological theory breaks down, for no accurate horoscope could be charted without considering all the planets and their supposed influence.

Twins

A constant source of embarrassment for astrologers is the birth of twins. Since they are born at exactly the same time and place, they should have the same destiny. Unfortunately, this is not the case, for experience shows us that two people who are born at the same time can live totally different lives. One may turn out to be very successful, while the other ends up a failure. The fact that twins do not live out the same lives shows another flaw in the theory.

Limited Perspective

A serious problem with astrology is its limited perspective. Astrology was born in an area close to the equator and did not take into consideration those living in latitudes where the zodiac signs do not appear for the same periods of time.

As Michel Gauquelin points out, "Astrology, begun in latitudes relatively close to the equator, made no provisions for the possibility that no planet may be in sight (in the higher latitudes) for several weeks in a row" (Michel Gauquelin, *The Cosmic Clocks*, Chicago, IL: Henry Regnery Co., 1967, p. 78).

This means those living in the higher latitudes in places such as Alaska, Norway, Finland and Greenland have no planetary influence in their lives, for it is almost impossible to calculate what point of the zodiac is rising on the horizon above the Arctic circle.

Since this is the case, one of the basic pillars of astrology now crumbles, as Van Buskirk points out, "Astrology can hardly be scientifically based on its own premise that the microcosm reflects the influence of the macrocosm, when one of the microcosms (man) above the 66th latitude is left uninfluenced by the cosmos" (Michael Van Buskirk, op. cit., p. 9).

No Scientific Verification

Probably the most damaging criticism that can be leveled at astrological prediction is the fact that its scientific value is nil. Paul Couderc, astronomer at the Paris Observatory, concluded after examining the horoscopes of 2,817 musicians:

> The position of the sun has absolutely no musical significance. The musicians are born throughout the entire year on a chance basis. No sign of the zodiac or fraction of a sign favors or does not favor them.
>
> We conclude: The assets of scientific astrology are equal to zero, as is the case with commercialized astrology. This is perhaps unfortunate, but it is a fact (Paul Couderc, L'Astrologie, "Que Sais-je?" 508; 3rd ed.; Paris: Presses Universitaires de France, 1961, pp. 86-89, cited by John Warwick Montgomery, Principalities and Powers, p. 106).

The statistics to support the predictive claims of astrologers are simply not there.

Incorrect Time of Reckoning

Another major problem with astrology concerns the fact that horoscopes are cast from the time of birth, not from the time of conception. Since all the hereditary factors are determined at conception, it should logically follow that the planets could begin influencing the person's destiny immediately after conception.

The problem is, of course, trying to accurately determine when conception took place, which is nearly impossible. However, if the planets do exert an influence over a person's fate, it should start at the time of conception rather than the time of birth.

The Shifting Constellations

Astrology is unscientific because of the fact of the precession or the shifting of constellations. Boa elaborates on this problem:

The early astronomers were not aware of precession and therefore failed to take it into account in their system. The twelve signs of the zodiac originally correspond with the twelve constellations of the same names. But due to precession, the constellations have shifted about 30 degrees in the last 2,000 years. This means that the constellation of Virgo is now in the sign of Libra, the constellation of Libra is now in the sign of Scorpio and so on. Thus, if a person is born on September 1, astrologers would call him a Virgo (the sign the sun is in at that date), but the sun is actually in the constellation Leo at that date. So there are two different zodiacs: one which slowly moves (the sidereal zodiac) and one which is stationary (the tropical zodiac). Which zodiac should be used? (Kenneth Boa, *Cults, World Religions, and You*, Wheaton, IL: Victor Books, 1977, pp. 124-125)

Furthermore, no constellation *ever* recurs. As Koch points out, "The most weighty factor is the astronomer's objection that no constellation in the sky ever recurs. Hence, astrological interpretations lack every basis of comparison. Hence, solstitial horoscopy rests on presuppositions which are scientifically untenable" (Kurt Koch, *Christian Counseling and Occultism*, Grand Rapids: Kregel Publishers, 1973, p. 94).

The Bible and Astrology

The Bible warns people against relying on astrologers and astrology:

You are wearied with your many counsels; let now the astrologers, those who prophesy by the stars, those who predict by the new moons, stand up and save you from what will come upon you. Behold, they have become like stubble; fire burns them; they cannot deliver themselves from the power of the flame . . . there is none to save you (Isaiah 47:13-15).

Other warnings can be found in such verses as Jeremiah 10:2: "Learn not the way of the heathen, and be not dismayed at the signs of heaven; for the heathen are dismayed at them" (KJV). Elsewhere, the Scripture says, "And beware, lest you lift up your eyes to heaven and see the sun and the moon and the stars, all the host of heaven, and be drawn away and worship them and serve them" (Deuteronomy 4:19).

The Book of Daniel gives us a comparison between the astrologers and those dedicated to the true and living God. Chapter 1, verse 20 reveals that Daniel and his three friends would be ten times better in matters of wisdom and understanding than the astrologers because they served the living and true God rather than the stars. When the king had a dream, the astrologers could not give an explanation for it, but rather God alone had the answer, for it is only He who can reveal the future (see Daniel 2:27,28).

The Scriptures make it clear that any type of astrological practice is severely condemned by God, for it attempts to understand the future through occultic means rather than through God's divinely inspired Word. The fatalistic approach of astrology, which says our lives are determined by the stars, is contradicted by Scripture, which holds us responsible for our destiny. Astrology and Christianity are simply incompatible.

Dangers of Astrology

There are some very real dangers in trying to live your life by a horoscope.

First is the attempt to try to run your life by following along in astrology. Since it is apparent a great deal of astrology has no basis in reality, you run the risk of great loss.

There can be the loss of money, both of what you may spend on astrology and what the astrologers may recommend for you to do. They may recommend you invest now, buy later, don't purchase this, etc. These recommended investments are no more certain than a fortune cookie, and you could suffer considerable financial loss.

Second, a person who continually tries to live his life by a horoscope can become very depressed as he begins to see life as fatalistic, predetermined since his birth, with no opportunity to break free. Women have even refused the medical advice of induced labor for a late pregnancy in order to have their baby born later, so as to be an Aquarius, for example.

> There is something pitiable about a lady I know who resides in a part of Europe not known for sophisticated medical practices and who refused to have the two-and-a-half-week-late birth of her child induced because she wanted him to be an Aquarius instead of whatever comes before that. I hope that the child suffers no unfortunate consequences (Samuel Hux, *The Humanist*, May/June 1978, "Parawhatsit: A Certain Incapacity to Appreciate the World," p. 32).

Why Do People Believe in Astrology?

If astrology is both unscientific and unbiblical, why do so many people believe in it?

One answer would be that it sometimes works, as one book on astrology attests: "When the late astrological genius, Grant Lewi, was asked why he believed in astrology, his blunt answer, 'I believe in it because it works.' This is as good an answer as any . . . we say that astrology works because it is based on natural law"

(Joseph Polansky, *Sun Sign Success*, New York: Warner/Destiny Books, 1977, p. 35).

There is a much better explanation for the so-called accuracy of astrological predictions. If one reads a horoscope, even in a cursory manner, he will be struck with the general and ambiguous nature of the statements, which can be pointed to as fulfilling anything and everything. *Time Magazine* observed:

> There are so many variables and options to play with that the astrologer is always right. Break a leg when your astrologer told you the signs were good, and he can congratulate you on escaping what might have happened had the signs been bad. Conversely, if you go against the signs and nothing happens, the astrologer can insist that you were subconsciously careful because you were forewarned (*Time Magazine*, March 21, 1969, p. 56).

The suggestive aspect also needs to be taken into consideration, as Koch has pointed out: "The person who seeks advice from an astrologer comes with a certain readiness to believe in the horoscope. This predisposition leads to an autosuggestion to order his life according to the horoscope, and thus contribute to its fulfillment" (Kurt Koch, *Occult and Christian Counseling*, op. cit., p. 95).

Astrology is bankrupt both biblically and scientifically. Since it is fatalistic in its approach, it rules out the free choice of each of us, leaving man merely as a cog in the cosmic machinery. This view of reality is at odds with Scripture, which indicates all of us have both the capacity and responsibility to choose which road in life we will take.

Astrology would deny us that choice and therefore must be rejected. The Scriptures show us a better way of looking into the future, seeing that God has already told us what the future holds for each of us and for our planet.

Cartomancy (Tarot Cards)

Cartomancy forecasts the future by means of using cards. The elaborately illustrated cards used in this technique are called tarot cards. Supposedly these cards hold the secrets to the future.

Those who use the cards extol their virtues:

The tarot is one of the most wonderful of human inventions. Despite all the outcries of philosophers, this pack of pictures, in which destiny is reflected as a mirror with multiple facets, remains so vital and exercises so irresistible an attraction on imaginative minds that it is hardly possible that austere critics who speak in the name of an exact but uninteresting logic should ever succeed in abolishing its employment (Grillot de Givry, *Witchcraft, Magic and Alchemy*, New York: Dover Publications, 1971, p. 280).

Wheatly offers this explanation:

Telling fortunes by cards is at the present day probably the most popular method of predicting a person's future.

There are two distinct types of pack: the tarot, or major arcana, which consists of twenty-two pictorial cards, none of which has any obvious relation to the others; and the minor arcana, which originally had fifty-six cards (in modern times reduced to fifty-two) divided into four suits. The suits, now diamonds, hearts, spades and clubs, were originally coins, cups, swords and staffs, which represented respectively commerce, spirituality, war and agriculture. In the old packs the fourteenth card in each suit was the Knight, who has since been dropped or, if one prefers, merged with Knave, who represents the squire of the Lord (King) and Lady (Queen).

The origin of both packs is lost in mystery. Some

writers have stated that the tarot is the Book of Thoth, the God of Wisdom of the Egyptians; others connect it with the twenty-two paths of the Hebrew Cabala, and still others assert that cards were introduced into western Europe by the Bohemians (Dennis Wheatly, *The Devil and All His Works*, New York: American Heritage Press, 1971, p. 62).

Those who turn to tarot readings are often insecure about the future. Not content to trust in the providence of God, they anxiously seek forbidden knowledge about the future in the hopes that such knowledge will enable them to escape some impending doom or fate.

There is nothing scientific about tarot cards. Although fantastic claims have been made for their powers through the centuries, no one has been able to produce significant evidence that such readings are reliable. While we would agree that the majority of tarot readings are completely fictitious, and depend more on the medium's ability to guess human nature than on spirit guides, there are some readings that appear to be genuinely supernatural.

Since these readings invariably lead a person away from the God of the Bible, and attempt to invade areas of knowledge God has determined should remain secret, we must conclude that they are demonic.

As Christians we can remain confident and peaceful, knowing that God is in full control of our unseen future. Jesus Christ is the only answer for one who is anxious about his future. He said:

But if God so arrays the grass of the field, which is alive today and tomorrow is thrown into the furnace, will He not much more do so for you, O men of little faith? Do not be anxious then, saying, "What shall we eat?" or "What shall we drink?" or "With what shall we clothe ourselves?" For all of these things the Gentiles eagerly seek; for your heavenly Father knows that you need all these things. But seek first His kingdom and His righteousness; and all these things shall be added to you. Therefore do not be anxious for tomorrow; for tomorrow will care for itself. Each day has enough trouble of its own (Matthew 6:30-34).

Crystal Gazing

Walk into any shopping mall when they are hosting a New Age festival and you will see booths set up with every imaginable form of occultism and divination. At least one booth will have a perfectly shaped sphere of highly polished crystal mounted on a pedestal. What is commonly called a crystal ball is no longer the spoof of old black and white movies. It has reemerged in the twentieth century as a profit-making business prop for the self-proclaimed fortune-teller.

Crystal gazing is a form of scrying, which means "seeing." The gazer is called the scryer and the tool of the trade can include anything from crystal balls to tea leaves. We have grouped crystal balls, mirrors and water gazing (usually in a silver bowl) together since this form of scrying relies upon the image perceived in the object. Other forms of scrying will be analyzed later.

Crystalmancy is another term used for divining through a crystal ball. Hydromancy is the proper term for gazing in a bowl or pool of water.

The crystal does not have to be a ball, as some are egg-shaped or even in the rough form of raw quartz. The professional crystal ball may be tinted pink, green, blue or white and may be transparent or translucent. Crystal gazers are often portrayed as passing their hands over the crystal in a preparation ceremony, which is said to "magnetize" the crystal (cf., *Man, Myth and Magic*, Cavendish, NY: Marshal, 1983, p. 2506).

Most crystal gazers claim to see clouded images in

the sphere that may be interpreted by its color or it may sharpen into a picture. They rarely claim to see supernatural beings, unless the scryer is a medium, who usually claims contact with departed spirits through the ball.

Mirror, Glass and Water Gazing

Mirror gazers use mirrors, glass or still water as "mirrors of the future." Sometimes these methods are used to find lost objects.

Gazing is an ancient method of divination. The one gazing into the mirror supposedly enters a state of clairvoyance where he can see events and things happening in the present or the future, regardless of distance from the diviner. When it is used to find lost objects, sometimes a piece of glass or a quartz stone will be used for gazing. It has been well documented that a similar method of glass-looking was used by Joseph Smith, Jr., founder of the Mormon Church. He was arrested and convicted in 1826 of glass-looking for finding buried treasure (cf., *Joseph Smith and the Occult*, Jude 3 Missions, P. O. Box 1901, Orange, CA 92668).

Mirror gazing has no foundation in Christianity or science. Rather than being a "window on the future," it is most often just the product of good guessing and a rich imagination on the part of the diviner. In a few cases, genuine occultic involvement appears to take place.

In either kind of instance the customer is seeking help from a medium or diviner. Throughout Scripture God condemns such practitioners and those who frequent them. They claim to speak for God but are actually frauds.

They see falsehood and lying divination who are saying, "The LORD declares," when the LORD has not sent them; yet they hope for the fulfillment of their word. Did you not see a false vision and speak a lying divination when you said, "The LORD declares," but it is not I who have spoken? Therefore, says the Lord GOD, "Because you have spoken falsehood and seen a lie, therefore behold, I am against you," declares the Lord GOD (Ezekiel 13:6-8).

Dreams

Everyone dreams, but not everyone remembers what he dreams and even fewer people believe in dreams as a source of guidance. Dreams are the activity of the subconscious mind during sleep. They appear as mental images and are often disjointed and meaningless. Occasionally, they represent an internal desire or need.

In the supernatural realm dreams can be used of God or they can be used for divination, which is forbidden by God. In the Old Testament times God spoke to individuals through dreams. Some of the more popular accounts about inspired dreams are Jacob's ladder (Genesis 28:12), the famine in Egypt (Genesis 41:1-36), Solomon choosing wisdom (1 Kings 3:3-15), Daniel's four beasts (Daniel 7:1-28), Joseph to marry Mary (Matthew 1:20,21), Joseph, Mary and Jesus to flee to Egypt (Matthew 2:13) and Pilate's wife concerning Jesus (Matthew 27:19).

God said he would sometimes speak to His people through dreams (Numbers 12:6; Joel 2:28). But the Bible sends forth the unmistakable message that we are not to seek omens or interpret dreams symbolically as our guide. Deuteronomy 13:1-5 sets forth God's condemnation of false dreamers who say their dreams were from Him, when in fact they were not. Jeremiah repeats this warning (23:25-32) and gives us insight into why dreams are not to be followed (29:8). The dreams they were receiving were from natural causes, the result of Nebuchadnezzar's repression of Israel, they were not from God. The dreamers falsely told Israel to serve Babylon (27:9) and were closely linked to divination in both passages.

The Freudian school of psychology has published a library of books on dream interpretation. His theory that dreams reveal unfulfilled desires and suppressed wishes has been discredited and hotly debated by many prominent psychologists. The Freudian interpretation was mainly sexual and aggressive in nature.

This opened the door for just as dubious literature to pour forth from the modern occultists who see dreams as a method of divination. Like Freud, they look for symbolic meaning behind the details of a dream. Their books are filled with omens and other contradictory interpretations.

Dream interpretation in psychoanalysis or divining can be dangerous on another level. It is quite deceptive in what it implants in the person's mind. If, for example, a dream interpreter tells the dreamer what his suppressed desire is or what his future holds for love, hatred, lust or adultery, then the person may go forth believing that is what is, since it is what he dreamed. To interpret that he hates his father may open the door to actual resentment against his father for no good cause. To interpret loving someone other than his wife may lead to divorce, adultery and a wrecked household.

To say that all dreams or any random dream is from God is to be pretentious. This, perhaps, is why God gave such stern warnings about dream interpretation in the Bible: "You shall not listen to the words of that prophet or that dreamer of dreams; for the LORD your God is testing you to find out if you love the LORD your God with all your heart and with all your soul" (Deuteronomy 13:3).

Numerology

Divining through numerology is an ancient practice that is based upon two premises. The first is the theory that numbers are directly associated with the real essence of a being. The second is that names and birth dates are universally controlled by a cosmic force that reveals the character of the person as well as his course in life.

Harper's Encyclopedia of Mystical and Paranormal Experience (San Francisco: Harper, 1991) sheds more light upon this:

> Numerology [is] a system of divination and magic based upon the concept that the universe is constructed in a mathematical pattern, and that all things may be expressed in numbers, which correspond to vibrations. By reducing names, words, birth dates, and birthplaces to numbers, a person's personality, destiny, and fortune may be determined (p. 409).

> Numerologists believe that one's full name given at birth is the expression of the vibratory forces of the universe, which determine one's character and destiny. Changing one's name can alter these factors, but several years supposedly are required for the vibrational patterns to readjust.

> Various formulae exist for detailed name analysis. Adding up vowels reveals one's 'heart's desire' or 'soul's urge'; adding up consonants reveals aspects of one's personality. The frequency of various letters determines the karmic lessons to be faced in life. The sum of the month, day, and year of birth tells the birth path, or the general direction of one's life. The sum of one's full name and birth date equals a power number, which acts as a beacon to guide one through life (p. 410).

Numerologists have attempted to make a biblical case for their practice by pointing to the number of the beast (666) in Revelation 13:18. They also point to the usage of significant numbers in the Bible to justify their practice, like the often used numbers of 3, 7, 10, 12 and 40.

This attempt at drawing a parallel with the frequent numbers of Scripture and divining by numerology is a misuse of the Bible. The biblical incident of attaching the number 666 to the name of the beast, in Revelation 13:18, is not the same as numerology. It is merely used to identify the beast, not to describe his character, birth date, and birthplace in relationship to a cosmic force. Dr. Henry Morris cautions Christians against using numbers as a way to place special significance upon doctrine, "Numbers cannot be used to teach doctrine, only to illustrate what is already in doctrine" (*Many Infallible Proofs*, Los Altos, CA: CLP Publishers, 1974, p. 319).

The Christian scholar, Dr. Oswald T. Allis, wrote that numerology complicates Scripture instead of clarifying it:

> In recent years the name of Ivan Panin has been connected with a most elaborate attempt to find numerical significance in every word and letter in the Bible. But his system is far too complicated to commend itself to the careful student. The Bible does not have an intricate numerical pattern which only a mathematical expert can discover. The strict and obvious meaning of words—and this applies to numbers—should be adhered to unless it is quite plain that some further meaning is involved. We know that the souls that were on the ship which was wrecked at Malta numbered two hundred seventy-six (Acts 27:37). Why this was the number we do not know, and it would be idle to try to find a mysterious or mystical meaning in this simple historical fact (*Baker's Theological Dictionary*, E. F. Harrison, Editor, Grand Rapids: Baker Book House, 1960, p. 381).

There is no parallel between the biblical usage of

numbers and the numerology as used by diviners. Numerologists have jeopardized their system by juggling and manipulating numbers to force a preconceived conclusion based upon a faulty world view. There is no consistency in their system, which makes suspect their foundation. If their world is mathematically arranged, but the inconsistency of the pattern denies this, then it is devoid of truth. Each new method of calculation devised by a numerologist disproves their theory all the more because it is a self-admission that numerology does not work, otherwise they would not have to invent a new formula of calculation.

Wayward theories that deceive the masses only end in failure and destruction. On the surface a system may appear viable, but underneath, its foundation is corrupt. Solomon said, "There is a way which seems right to a man, but its end is the way of death" (Proverbs 16:25).

Oracles

A number of religious books are used by diviners in the belief that there is some kind of esoteric power that accompanies the book. Whether it is the Bible, Koran, Virgil's *Aeneid*, *I Ching* or a modern oracle, the methodology is the same. They open the book at random and follow for guidance what their finger happens to fall upon.

I Ching or *The Book of Changes*

This ancient book of Chinese divination supposedly originated before Confucius, during the reign of King Wen (1200 B.C.). Commentaries were added to it through the years by Confucius and his disciples. It has been regularly consulted in Oriental cultures for national direction right down to World War II, when the Japanese commanders consulted it for military moves.

Psychologist Carl Jung was so influenced by it that he wrote the preface for the first English translation.

The Book of Changes is the English equivalent for *I Ching*. It is based upon the philosophical dualism of yang and yin. These two equal forces interplay in the events of everyday life. Through making the correct decisions one can establish harmony with yang and yin in the midst of constant change.

The way one makes his decision is based upon a complex system of casting yarrow sticks and interpreting the pattern of the fallen sticks by matching them to hexagrams that identify what *The Book of Changes* says. Coins, cards, dice or stones may be used in place of yarrow sticks. In this case three objects are tossed six times and their pattern is recorded each time. The fixed pattern is matched to the hexagrams for the answer to the question asked.

Runes

The use of runes is a different type of oracle and is passed down from the alphabet of Northern Europe. The rune alphabet has twenty-four symbols and one blank symbol. They were originally used for divination and to ward off evil.

They are somewhat different than yes or no oracles. They are supposed to describe a circumstance and help the person react accordingly by steering one through a problem.

The runes can be professionally manufactured or homemade from stones or wood. They are placed in a bag and carried with the diviner. When the need arises for consultation the diviner simply reaches into the bag and draws one rune for advice. There are positive and negative interpretations of each rune, depending upon whether it was withdrawn face-up or face-down. The alternative three-rune method is to meditate upon the problem and draw three runes. The first draw represents the past, the second is the present, and the third is the future.

Books of Oracles

Other books have been used as oracles to replace *I Ching*. A new Western book is *The Oracle Within* by New Age writer Dick Sutphen (Malibu: Pocket Books, 1991). He has written 250 "life-guiding" messages from which the reader opens the book at random and receives the message for his problem or question. If further clarification is needed, just toss a coin three times and your inner consciousness will guide you to a new message through interpreting the tossed coin.

Bible Roulette

We have borrowed the term "Bible roulette" from the late Dr. Walter R. Martin, who referred to this form of divination in this way. The diviner prays or meditates and then opens the Bible at random, usually with closed eyes, and points to a verse on the page. Whatever the finger lands upon is supposed to be a message. Bible diviners do this three times to get a complete message. The fallacy Dr. Martin would point out, with tongue-in-cheek, is "What do you do if your three passages are Matthew 27:5, Luke 10:37, and John 13:27?—He went away and hanged himself . . . go and do the same . . . what you do, do quickly."

It becomes futile to think that one can be guided by such a method. The Bible was never intended to play roulette or to use as a source of divination. Its purpose is to give us doctrine, reproof, correction, and instruction in righteousness (2 Timothy 3:16).

Ouija Boards

One of the most popular occultic devices in the

world today is the Ouija board. What is the Ouija board and what does it claim to do? *The Dictionary of Mysticism* has this to say concerning the Ouija board:

> An instrument for communication with the spirits of the dead. Made in various shapes and designs, some of them used in the sixth century before Christ. The common feature of all its varieties is that an object moves under the hand of the medium, and one of its corners, or a pointer attached to it, spells out messages by successively pointing to letters of the alphabet marked on a board which is part of the instrument (Frank Gaynor, ed., *Dictionary of Mysticism*, New York: Citadel Press, n.d., p. 132).

The Ouija board is considered by some as nothing more than a party game. Others believe that using it can reveal hidden things in the subconscious. Still others believe that, while the communications are produced supernaturally, the supernatural source is demonic rather than from "beyond the grave." One Christian authority in the occult, Kurt Koch, has strong feelings on the subject.

> Psychologists would have us believe that the game is harmless. They hold that it is only a matter of bringing to light things hidden in our subconscious minds. This view can swiftly be refuted. With the Ouija board, revelations from the hidden past and predictions about the future are made. These things could not possibly be stored in our subconscious minds (Kurt Koch, *Occult ABC*, Grand Rapids, MI: Kregel Publications, n.d., p. 152).

Our convictions concerning the Ouija board agree exactly with those of noted cult and occult observer Edmond Gruss.

> The Ouija board should be seen as a device which sometimes actually makes contact with the supernatural for several reasons:

- The content of the messages often goes beyond that which can be reasonably explained as coming from the conscious or subconscious mind of the operator. Examples of such are presented in Sir William F. Barrett's *On the Threshold of the Unseen* (pp. 176-189), and in the experiences of Mrs. John H. Curran, related in the book *Singer in the Shadows*.

- The many cases of "possession" after a period of Ouija board use also support the claim that supernatural contact is made through the board. Psychics and parapsychologists have received letters from hundreds of people who have experienced "possession" (an invasion of their personalities). Rev. Donald Page, a well-known clairvoyant and exorcist of the Christian Spiritualist Church, is reported as saying that most of his "possession" cases "are people who have used the Ouija board," and that "this is one of the easiest and quickest ways to become 'possessed' " (*Man, Myth and Magic*, number 73, after p. 2060). While Page views these "possessions" as caused by disincarnate entities, the reality of possession is still clear. The Christian sees the invader as an evil spirit (demon).

- The board has been subjected to tests which support supernatural intervention. The testing of the board was presented in an article by Sir William Barrett, in the September 1914 *Proceedings of the American Society for Psychical Research* (pp. 381-894). The Barrett report indicated that the board worked efficiently with the operators blindfolded, the board's alphabet rearranged and its surface hidden from the sight of those working it. It worked with such speed and accuracy under these tests that Barrett concluded:

   Reviewing the results as a whole, I am convinced of their supernormal character, and that we have here an exhibition of some intelligent, disincarnate agency, mingling with the personality of one or more of the sitters and guiding their muscular movements (p. 394).

   In his book, *On the Threshold of the Unseen*, Barrett

referred to these same experiences and stated, "Whatever may have been the source of the intelligence displayed, it was absolutely beyond the range of any normal human faculty" (p. 181). Similar statements could be multiplied.

The fact remains that the Ouija board works. Much phenomena is certainly through conscious and subconscious activity, but that some is of supernatural character must be accepted (Edmond Gruss, *Cults and Occult in the Age of Aquarius*, Philipsburg, NJ: 1980, pp. 115-116).

The magician, Danny Korem, feels there is nothing supernatural connected with the Ouija board.

I have never witnessed, read, or heard of a credible report of something of a supernatural nature taking place through the use of the Ouija board. I have seen, heard, and read, however, of many negative experiences that have entrapped people who have sought knowledge with a Ouija board. If you own a Ouija board or some similar diversion, my advice is to destroy it and never encourage others to tinker with such devices. You never know what emotional disturbances might be triggered in yourself or others through their use.

If you are still unconvinced and believe that some power might be manifested, then one should utilize the following procedure. The letters should be scattered at random, without your knowledge of their position, around the board; a bag should be placed over your head to prevent your viewing the board; and the entire letter-finding task should be viewed by a qualified magician, who would verify your lack of vision. Then and only then, if there are forces at work, will they produce something literate let alone prophetic. To save you the time and effort, let me add that this has already been tried with negative results (Danny Korem and Paul Meier, *The Fakers*, Grand Rapids, MI: Baker Book House, 1980, pp. 70-71).

Even though the above writers see different methods at work, they both draw the same conclusion that the Ouija board is not a plaything. It is another tool often used by Satan to get people to look somewhere else besides to Jesus Christ for the answers. It is dangerous because it is based upon the same ideas as New Age channeling. The person who works the board may be able to spell out words by natural or subconscious means, but as a tool for divination, the person is expecting a force other than his own to move the device. God will not oblige the board workers, which leaves only one other source for guidance—the demonic realm.

Palmistry (Chiromancy)

Palmistry, or chiromancy, is the art of divination from the shape and markings of the hands and fingers. A proper interpretation of these signs supposedly can be used to forecast the future. It is not to be confused with chirology, which is the scientific study of the development of the shape and lines of the hand, or with graphology, which is handwriting analysis.

Kurt Koch explains chiromancy:

Here we have fortune-telling by study of the hands. The hand is divided into areas and lines. There is a lunar mountain, the Venus belt, the Martian plain, and areas for spirit, fortune, success, fame, imagination, will and sensuousness. Further, there are four lines which dominate the surface of the palm: the head line, the heart line, the profession line and the life line. From these indications palmists claim to divine and foretell the future (Kurt Koch, *Christian Counseling and Occultism*, Grand Rapids, MI: Kregel Publications, 1972, p. 85).

Unfortunately, palmistry suffers from the same types of verification problems as does astrology. There is no testable, scientific evidence that it works. Lack of documentation and testability have led to the scientific community to brand it as mere superstition. The so-called examples of palmistry being able to predict the future have never been substantiated as being right any more often than pure chance would already allow.

As far as trying to justify palmistry from the Bible is concerned, the cause is a hopeless one. The out-of-context verses used by some have nothing to do with palm reading. Moreover, the Scriptures speak loudly and clearly against trying to foretell the future using any form of divination. The following Scripture would apply to palmistry:

> There shall not be found among you anyone who makes his son or daughter pass through the fire, one who uses divination, one who practices witchcraft, or one who interprets omens, or a sorcerer, or one who casts a spell, or a medium, or a spiritist, or one who calls up the dead. For whoever does these things is detestable to the LORD; and because of these detestable things the LORD your God will drive them out before you (Deuteronomy 18:10-12).

Psychometry

Psychometry can also be classed in the area of fortune-telling. The idea behind psychometry is summed up in the *Dictionary of Mysticism:*

> The psychic faculty of certain persons to divine events connected with material objects when in close contact with the latter. The material objects are considered to be acting as catalysts for the PSI faculty. Occultists call it "reading or seeing" with the inner sight (Frank Gaynor, ed., *Dictionary of Mysticism*, New York: Citadel Press, n.d., p. 148).

Psychometry consists of a person holding some material object of another in his hands and having the ability to make statements and identify characteristics of the owner of the article. He may even foretell part of the future of the owner.

Psychometry has no place in the Christian's life. We are not to depend on mediums and their paraphernalia for help in this world. Rather than depending on other men who are fallible and serving Satan rather than the Lord God, we should depend on the Holy Spirit, whose specific job is to guide us in God's will. Christians can avail themselves of the only true "medium," the Holy Spirit.

> And I will ask the Father, and He will give you another Helper, that He may be with you forever; that is the Spirit of truth, whom the world cannot receive, because it does not behold Him or know Him (John 14:16,17).

> But the Helper, the Holy Spirit, whom the Father will send in My name, He will teach you all things, and bring to your remembrance all that I said to you (John 14:26).

> And in the same way the Spirit also helps our weaknesses; for we do not know how to pray as we should, but the Spirit Himself intercedes for us with groanings too deep for words; and He who searches the hearts knows what the mind of the Spirit is, because He intercedes for the saints according to the will of God (Romans 8:26,27).

We have no need of psychometry or any other occultic practice if we have the Holy Spirit within us.

Radiestesia—Rods and Pendulums

Radiestesia is the practice of medical diagnosis, discovery of lost objects or missing persons, telepathy, or knowing a future event through the use of a divining rod, dowsing rod or pendulum. The usual theory is that the diviner acts as a conduit of energy and works the rod or pendulum through his subconscious mind. In some cases the pendulum or rod is used over a map to find missing persons, minerals, water or treasures.

Harper's Encyclopedia of Mystical and Paranormal Experience explains how dowsing and pendulums are used in divination:

> In Europe, Great Britain, and elsewhere, dowsing is sometimes used as a diagnostic tool in alternative medicine. A pendulum is suspended over the patient's body and "attuned" to healthy parts. As it is moved over unhealthy parts, the pendulum's movements change. The dowser also may ask questions and divine answers according to the rotation of the pendulum; clockwise for "yes," and counterclockwise for "no" (op. cit., p. 157).

One study on dowsing for water proved its unreliable characteristic:

> P. A. Ongley reported in the *New Zealand Journal of Science and Technology*, in 1948, that fifty-eight dowsers participated in tests devised to determine their ability to make the same spots they had indicated with their eyes open when their eyes were closed, to tell if buried bottles contained water, and otherwise give evidence of their purported powers. Their scores were on pure-chance levels. Seventeen other diviners who specialize in diverse fields were observed. As in the earlier experiments in France, seven illness detectors found twenty-five diseases in a patient who doctors said was healthy, and one diviner, whose eyes were bandaged, said the leg over which he worked had varicose veins. Actually it was an artificial limb (Milbourne Cristopher, *ESP, Seers and Psychics*, New York: Thomas Y. Crowell Co., p. 140).

Dowsers and pendulum diviners have tried to associate their work with the rod of Aaron in the Bible, citing how Moses used it to bring water out of the rock, and for other miracles. This is a misuse of the Bible, for Moses did not use the rod to locate things, including water. The Lord told Moses water was in the rock (Exodus 17:6), so the rod was not used to find it. Moses never used the rod of Aaron for diagnosis or to find things.

Scrying—Coffee, Tea or Wax

It seems that people will find any substance useful for divination. *Scrying* means "seeing," from which we get the word *descrying,* to observe or catch sight. The three items we will discuss here are coffee grounds, tea leaves and hot wax dropped in water.

In ancient Babylon the liver of a freshly killed animal was examined in much the same way as scrying exists today (Ezekiel 21:21). The dependence of Nebuchadnezzar upon divination is seen in this verse. He used three methods, one was consulting an idol, another was examining the liver, and the last was shaking a quiver with marked arrows to divine by the first to fall out. This shows his distrust of divination, since he had to use three methods to determine one decision.

The Divination Handbook by C. Q. Kennedy (New York: Signet Books, 1989) explains how coffee grounds are read:

> The coffee for this type of reading can be of any variety but is best prepared in a percolator or samovar or by a method that does not require a filter. Clean white porcelain or stoneware cups are best to use as the shapes can be more easily read. The person who requires the reading drinks the coffee, leaving a small amount, one or two sips at most, in the bottom of the cup. Swirl the contents of the cup slowly while concentrating on the question or questions. Allow the liquid to settle and study the formations of the grounds that cling to the sides of the cup (p. 46).

He then gives thirty-five suggested meanings for the formations.

Kennedy explains the similarity of tea leaf reading:

> Use Indian or British teas, since they have the largest leaves . . . Leave about a quarter of an inch of tea at the bottom of the cup after drinking it. Swirl the liquid around so the tea leaves are stirred up from the bottom and begin to cling to the sides of the cup, while concentrating on the question at hand (p. 204).

Wax divination, as explained by Kennedy, is quite different:

> With the question fixed in the querent's mind, the [hot] wax should be poured slowly into another brass bowl filled with ice-cold water. The wax will spread in thin layers, and within minutes, discernable shapes will form from which your answers can be read (p. 208).

Kennedy then gives suggested interpretations for the shapes of the wax formations.

This form of divination is similar to looking at the liver, as Nebuchadnezzar did in Ezekiel 21:21. When the animal would be slaughtered, the liver would be removed and examined. The various positions of markings on its surface were interpreted by their soothsayers. All practices of divination by soothsayers are forbidden by God (Deuteronomy 18:10-12; Micah 5:12).

Table Tipping

This form of divination was popularized in the mid-1800s through the Fox sisters and the spiritualist movement. The vogue ritual was easy to do and required nothing more than a table and like-minded friends. Being confined to households made it attractive to people who otherwise would not visit a medium or spiritist.

The Divination Handbook gives details about table tipping:

> Table tipping requires two participants; each sits comfortably on either side of a table (folding card tables are best for the purpose) and places their fingertips lightly on the edge of the table until they both sense a definite presence, usually through a strong, warm, tingling sensation that travels up through the fingertips and into the forearms. Before long, and without pushing, the table will tip or rise up and balance on two legs.

> Instruct the presence that it is to answer questions thus: one tip or bounce for yes, two for no. Immediately inquire of the spirit present whether or not it is of the Light, and if the answer is no, abandon the table for the moment and try again later when you are certain the presence has departed (op. cit., pp. 184-185).

It never ceases to amaze us the contradictions people believe. If Mr. Kennedy thinks that a spirit of darkness would tell the truth when asked if it is of the light, then he does not understand what a lying spirit is (1 Kings 22:22). Why does Mr. Kennedy think that a lying spirit will tell him the truth?

Debunkers have spoofed table tipping as fraudulent and explainable through natural means. The most incriminating evidence against table tipping was the public confession of Katie and Maggie Fox, founders of the Spiritism movement, when they admitted they used deception. Maggie Fox said the tapping noise from their table sittings was produced through the crackling of an abnormal joint in her toe (cf., Walter R. Martin, *Kingdom of the Cults*, Minneapolis: Bethany House Publishers, 1985, p. 229). Rather than her confession's dealing a final blow to table tipping or table tapping, the practice still continued after her admission.

Dr. Martin also warned of the dangers of spiritism,

calling it a "masquerade of demonic forces." It seems that demonic spirits are not respectful of fraudulent beginnings and will make contact with a person who is open to necromancy. All spiritism and necromancy is rejected by the people of God (Isaiah 8:19,20).

In conclusion, there are many different names for fortune-tellers or mediums. By whatever name, they are completely condemned by the Bible. God calls them detestable in Deuteronomy 18:11,12. One who practices such things was condemned to death under the Old Testament theocracy (Leviticus 20:27).

Such false prophets (Jeremiah 14:14) were sometimes called astrologers (Isaiah 47:13), mediums (Deuteronomy 18:11), diviners (Deuteronomy 18:14), magicians (Genesis 41:8), soothsayers (Isaiah 2:6), sorcerers (Acts 13:6,8, KJV), and spiritists (Deuteronomy 18:11).

The Lord God promises that someday he will "cut off sorceries from your hand, and you will have fortunetellers no more" (Micah 5:12).

6

New Age Occultism

The New Age Movement is vast and takes in a broad spectrum of concepts from the occult to Eastern philosophy and global transformation. We plan to deal with the specific healing and occultic practices in this chapter. For those who would like to have an overview of the philosophical and religious aspects of the New Age Movement, please see our chapter in *The Deceivers* (San Bernardino: Here's Life Publishers, 1992).

Some New Age occultism is only possible through modern technology. Other practices are borrowed from classical occultism and have been totally absorbed by New Agers. It is hard to find a person in some of the older practices who is not also in the New Age Movement.

The basic premises of New Age teachings are:

1. Their world view is monistic (all is one) or pan-

theistic (all is God). This oneness of all things is called Ultimate Reality.

2. The world and evil are not part of the Reality; therefore they are called an illusion, or maya, as the Hindus called it. Only spirit and good are the Reality, all else is illusion.

3. Man's nature is basically good, but his present karma prevents him from realizing his goodness.

4. Man is divine, God, or Christ within.

5. Man creates his own existence and is responsible for his current circumstances as well as what he creates for himself in the future.

6. Life is a perpetual cycle of reincarnation governed by the law of karma.

7. Salvation or release from the world (illusion) is achieved through becoming one with the One (monism) or becoming one with God (pantheism).

8. One or more New Age techniques may be used to achieve the oneness, which is called self-transformation.

9. Ultimately global transformation will be achieved when all humans undergo self-transformation.

All occult practices have this common denominator: They seek supernatural power outside of the God of the Bible. This may come in the form of claiming a supernatural power exists within man or contact with a supernatural power in the spirit-world.

One other note that may help us in understanding and dealing with New Agers is their concept of the spirituality of man. New Agers often say, "I am not this body," in an effort to show the spiritual side of man. It is a fallacy, however, to claim that the spiritual side is all there is to man, for without the body he has no proof of his existence.

Biblically, the body is a necessary part of man's being, as we see when God formed Adam from the dust of the ground (Genesis 2:7). Then God breathed "the breath of life" into Adam and he became a living soul (Genesis 2:7). Man is not complete if he is only a body, for the body without the spirit is dead (James 2:26). And man is incomplete when he is only spirit, thus the necessity of the bodily resurrection (Romans 8:11). Man was created as a material and spiritual entity, although the two are separated by death, they shall be reunited in the resurrection as the complete man in Christ (1 Corinthians 15:19-21).

The flaw in the New Age understanding concerning man is that the body is a temporary obstruction in our progression toward reunion with the cosmic energy. They view the body as an energy field (Ch'i, chakra, etc.) that is temporarily in disharmony with the greater Reality; so they devise techniques based on bringing the body back into harmony with the Ultimate Reality. The unscriptural foundation for the following techniques is rooted in their misconception of man and the universe.

A Course in Miracles

I have one of these books! R.F. IT IS BAD!

This three-volume book collection, entitled *A Course in Miracles*, has sold 250,000 sets worldwide and is available in six languages. The course has been accepted by some liberal Christian pastors on the basis that it has Christian jargon sprinkled throughout the text and was revealed by the spirit of Jesus.

The fact is it was channeled through a New Age psychologist, Dr. Helen Schucman, over an eight-year period. Dr. Schucman acted as a medium for the spirit that spoke to her. She claimed the "Voice" said it was Jesus and dictated words to her "mentally."

Some of the many unbiblical teachings in *A Course in Miracles* are designed to correct the "errors" of orthodox Christianity. Biblical terms are redefined to reinterpret the gospel message. The course claims to be an attitude-changing theory for raising a man's consciousness from the "guilt" of "thinking he is a sinner" to accepting the correct attitude about himself. The course presents pantheism, "God is in everything I see" (*Course*, 2:1), which is contrary to the God of the Scriptures, who is personal (Genesis 1:26) and distinct from His creation (Genesis 1:1; John 1:3; Colossians 1:16,17).

The sinfulness of man is denied: "I choose to see my brother's sinlessness. My sinlessness protects me from all harm" (*Course*, 2:1). Further, it says, "If sin is real, both God and you are not" (*Course*, 1:377). This is refuted in the biblical passages that tell us all people are held guilty of sin through Adam (Romans 5:12), all have sinned and fall short of God's glory (Romans 3:23), and there is none righteous, no not one (Psalm 14:3; Romans 3:10). He that denies he is a sinner is a liar, and makes God a liar (1 John 1:10).

The biblical nature of Jesus Christ is denied in *A Course in Miracles*. As with other gnostic groups, the "Christ" is not Jesus but is a spiritual principle Jesus acquired. The course says, "The name of Jesus is the name of one who was a man but saw the face of Christ in all his brothers and remembered God . . . And Christ needed his form that he might appear to men and save them from their own illusions" (*Course*, 3:83). The New Testament contains several statements that shred the fabric of gnosticism. The apostle John said, "Who is the liar but the one who denies that Jesus is the Christ? This is the antichrist" (1 John 2:22). With that we can see that Jesus did not see the "Christ" in all his brothers because

He is the Christ. He also declared himself as God. He did not just "remember" God; He was God incarnate (John 5:18; 8:58; 10:30; Revelation 1:8).

The blood atonement of Jesus for our sins is denied in *A Course in Miracles*. It says:

> Persecution frequently results in an attempt to justify the terrible misperception that God himself persecuted His own Son on behalf of salvation . . . [Jesus speaking] I have been correctly referred to as "the Lamb of God who taketh away the sins of the world, but those who represent the lamb as blood-stained do not understand the meaning of the symbol . . . Teach only love . . . If you interpret the crucifixion in any other way, you are using it as a weapon for assault rather than as the all for peace for which it was intended" (*Course*, 2:32,33,87).

The Bible clearly rejects such a shallow view and outright denial of Christ's blood atonement. He is the lamb slain from before the foundation of the world (Revelation 13:8). His blood is the way of forgiveness through grace (Ephesians 1:7; Colossians 1:14). Without the shedding of blood there is no remission of sins (Hebrews 9:22). His blood cleanses us of all sin, and as we ask Him for forgiveness, He is faithful and just to forgive us (1 John 1:7-9).

A Course in Miracles is the wrong course. It is a course in deception brought about through occultic spirit-channeling and only offers a course to eternal damnation in hell. "You formerly walked according to the course of this world, according to the prince of the power of the air, of the spirit that is now working in the sons of disobedience" (Ephesians 2:2).

Auras

Jesus said to let our light shine before men (Matthew 5:16). Was He talking about an aura? New Agers seem to think so and have used the nimbus (halo) over

Jesus in oil paintings as proof that auras were known by the "spiritually aware" artists in the church.

An aura is supposed to be a colored light or glow that radiates from a person to show their temperament or health condition. The occultic nature of auras is found in *Harpers Encyclopedia of Mystical and Paranormal Experience:*

> Clairvoyants see the aura as emanating from and interpreting the human body. Health and emotion show in various colors, energy patterns or breaks, and clear and cloudy spots. Physical health seems related to the part of the aura that is closest to the body, often called the vital body or etheric body ... From childhood Edgar Cayce saw colored fields around people, which he learned indicated their health, state of mind, and spiritual development (p. 4).

Books pour forth from the New Age presses for interpreting the colors of auras, but they are not consistent in their content. The variations are according to the whim of the writer.

Almost all believers in auras base their "proof" upon the work of Semyon Kirlian, a Russian technician, who accidentally photographed his fingers during an experiment with electrical charged plates in 1939. The result showed a strange corona (aura) emitting from the edges of his fingers. The story of his discovery made its way to the United States in the mid-1970s. Dr. Thelma Moss, of UCLA, popularized the technique by photographing "auras" of everything from hands to seeds.

The New Age movement picked up on the strange phenomenon and offered a number of hypotheses for the aura: photographed spirits, etheric bodies, nimbus, halo, aura, bioenergy fields, and so on.

A number of study groups experimented with Kir-

lian photography and found purely natural explanations for the "aura" image. *Smithsonian* magazine
offered this explanation in an interview:

> Gary Poock, who labors at the Man-Machine Systems
> Design Laboratory of the U. S. Naval Post-Graduate
> School in Monterey, California ... says that one needs
> real experience to obtain consistent results. "You are
> dealing with electrons and physics and film," he
> declares. "You can make a lot of mistakes. That's what
> happens in about 95 percent of the research." He and a
> collaborator, Paul W. Sparks, have identified at least thir-
> teen factors that can influence the Kirlian image,
> including voltage level, voltage pulse rate, moisture, at-
> mospheric gases, the internal force and angle of the
> object held against the film, and barometric pressure
> (April 1977, p. 111).

The article went on to say, "In conclusion: Kirlian
photography, if properly controlled, is an excellent way
to measure the moisture content of objects, period" (p.
112).

The New Agers, clairvoyants and psychics who
claim Kirlian photography is proof of auras have an un-
founded claim. What do we say about those who "see"
a light, nimbus or aura emitting from people?

In our research on this, Kurt Van Gorden has inter-
viewed psychics at several New Age festivals and
found conflicting reports about what is seen at the same
moment. At one point two ladies argued in front of him
about whether there was a red or blue aura. They see
what they want to see. Their experience is subjective,
unreliable, unconvincing, and unverifiable. We believe
they have deceived themselves by thinking they have a
special gift, when there is no evidence for such a gift.
Our advice is, "See to it that no one takes you captive
through philosophy and empty deception ... rather
than according to Christ" (Colossians 2:8).

Automatic Writing

This method of channeling information from a living, but distant, person or from a departed spirit is not new in occult circles. It has emerged in the New Age Movement as the means for several books by Alice Bailey (Lucis Trust), Jane Roberts (Seth series), and Ruth Montgomery (a noted psychic). Other forms of automatisms are automatic speaking, automatic painting and automatic music.

The *Encyclopedia of Occultism and Parapsychology* (Leslie A. Shepherd, editor, Detroit: Gail Research, 1984) explains how it is done:

> When the phenomena are produced during a state of trance or somnambulism, the agent may be entirely unconscious of his or her actions. On the other hand, the automatic writing may be executed while the agent is in a condition scarcely varying from the normal and quite capable of observing the phenomena in a critical spirit, though perhaps ignorant of a word in advance of what he is actually writing (p. 108).

The example for how a person is controlled has all the markings of demon activity. Stainton Moses wrote in *Spirit Identity* (1879):

> [In 1872] My right arm was seized about the middle of the forearm, and dashed violently up and down with a noise resembling that of a number of paviors at work. It was the most tremendous exhibition of unconscious muscular action I ever saw. In vain I tried to stop it. I distinctly felt the grasps, soft and firm, round my arm, and though perfectly possessed of senses and volition, I was powerless (ibid.).

What may excite people in the occult is frightening when analyzed by the Bible. The description above shows how contact with spirits can lead to demonic control. When Mr. Moses spoke of how he tried to stop his arm from writing, but couldn't, it is reminiscent of the demon-possessed boy in Mark 9:17-22 who was "thrown" into fire and water to destroy him. Jesus cast the demon out of the boy and freed him from its controlling force.

Biorhythm

Predicting the successful days in life and avoiding disastrous days has always been the trade of fortune-tellers. If one could invent a way to take it out of the gypsy wagon and place it in a high-tech setting that looks like a scientific analysis, then he could gain a new clientele that would normally scoff at the occult. This is the story of biorhythms. It was first conceived by Wilhelm Fliess, a German physician and friend of Sigmond Freud. It found little acceptance until the human potential movement popularized it in the 1970s. Now computerized biorhythm machines are vogue. You find them in airports, hotel lobbies and restaurants. A large number of Japanese businesses plan their ventures by biorhythms and several large American corporations have done the same.

Biorhythm plotting is a blend of astrology and numerology. It is believed that your birth date is tied in to planetary movement and a numeric life-cycle of twenty-three, twenty-eight and thirty-three days. It is explained in the *Encyclopedia of Occultism and Parapsychology:*

> The theory of biochemical phasing .. claims that human beings experience three major biological cycles which may be charted as: (1) a twenty-three day cycle of physical strength, energy, endurance, (2) a twenty-eight day cycle of emotional sensibility, intuition, creative ability, (3) a thirty-three day cycle of mental activity, reasoning, ambition.

Charts of these cycles indicate periods of maximum

or minimum potential in any of the three cycles, as well as critical dates of stress when two or three of the cycles intersect (p. 151).

The scientific community has been amused at the biorhythm fad. The coincidence of Judy Garland and Marilyn Monroe committing suicide during their "low points" is by chance. This falls into the category of, "If I had not believed it, I would not have seen it." What the biorhythm experts do not discuss is the people who commit suicide on their "high peaks." There is no consistency to the theory and it refutes itself by the failures through controlled study (cf., Henry Gordon, *Extra-Sensory Deception*, Buffalo, NY: Prometheus Books, 1987, p. 79).

The biorhythm chart has replaced the horoscope for some people. Why? Simply because some of your most critical days on your biorhythm chart will be contradicted by your horoscope. Both horoscopes and biorhythms are "monthly prognosticators" and are equally condemned in Isaiah 47:13 (KJV).

Chakras

A chakra is an energy point as defined by yogis in Hinduism. New Agers will commonly say there are seven chakras in the human body, but some opt for eight or ten. *Harper's Encyclopedia of Mystical and Paranormal Experiences* says:

Chakra is Sanskrit for "wheel." Chakras are said to be shaped like multicolored lotus petals or spoked wheels that whirl at various speeds as they process energy. Chakras are described in Hindu and Buddhist yogic literature . . .

The health of chakras is diagnosed by clairvoyance, by energy scans with the hands, and by dowsing with a pendulum. Clairvoyants say that health disturbances often manifest in the aura, and thus in the chakras, months and sometimes years before they manifest in the physical body.

There are seven major chakras and hundreds of minor ones ... The chakras are connected to each other and to the body through the nadis, channels of subtle energy. There are thousands of nadis, of which three are the most important ...

The seven major etheric chakras are the root, the sacral, the solar plexus, the heart, the throat, the brow, and the crown:

1. The root (muladara) is located at the base of the spine and is the seat of kundalini. It is concerned with self-preservation, one's animal nature, taste and smell ...

2. The sacral (svadhisthana) lies near the genitals and governs sexuality and reproduction ... It influences overall health ...

3. The solar plexus (manipurna) rests just above the navel ... It is associated with the emotions, and is the point where astral energy enters the etheric field ...

4. The heart (anahata) ... is located midway between the shoulder blades, in the center of the chest ... It is linked to higher consciousness and unconditional love.

5. The throat (visuddha) ... is associated with creativity and self expression and the search for truth ... This chakra is associated with certain states of expanded consciousness.

6. The brow (ajna), located between the eyebrows, is called the third eye for its influence over psychic sense and spiritual enlightment ...

7. The crown (sahasrara) whirls just above the top of the head ... It reveals the individual's level of conscious evolution. The crown cannot be activated until all the other chakras are refined and balanced; when activated it brings supreme enlightment and cosmic consciousness (op. cit., pp. 86-87).

There is no evidence for the existence of the chakras. Those in the New Age Movement who use crystals and wands for healing through the chakras disprove their own system. They are forever "energizing" crystals or purchasing new crystals because a healing failed. Have they ever considered that the chakras are not there and that alone explains the continued illness of a patient?

This mystical theory of the body is unbiblical and leads people away from God. The Bible clearly shows that supernatural healing comes only from faith and prayer in the true God (James 5:13), who does all things according to His will (James 4:15).

Channeling and Akashic Records

Channeling is a generic New Age term for any number of ways a living person or a spirit-being communicates through a medium. Trance channeling is what most people associate with the term. This occurs when the medium slips into a trance-like state (altered state of consciousness) and allows a spirit (angel, deity, departed human, etc.) to speak through his body. Sometimes the message is vocal (automatic speaking) and sometimes it is a silent (mental) communication. Other ways of channeling are automatic writing, "liquid light" (Ballinger), word appearances (Blavatsky), sleep (Casey), dreams, visions, Ouija boards (Roberts), or apparitions.

There is not a lot of difference between a channeler and a spiritist, except the spiritist uses props and usually sticks with necromancy. Channelers are found in all parts of the United States and often advertise for business. One Florida channeler, Jack Parsel, has a two-year waiting list at $93 an hour. Gerry Bowman used to have a radio show on KIEV, a Los Angeles talk-radio station, where he channeled the apostle John "live" on the air.

Another channeler, speaking for the Virgin Mary, said John F. Kennedy was still in purgatory for mishandling the missile crisis in Cuba (cf., Russell Chandler, *Understanding the New Age*, Dallas: Word Publishers, 1991, p. 68).

The Akashic Records are supposed to be an information resource for spiritists, mediums and channelers, from which they can obtain past, present and future information on mankind's existence. These records contain lucid representations in a cosmic energy form of every personal action in life. Channelers often consult the records for information on reincarnation and past-life recall.

The Akashic Records do not have all the truth, though. There are ample cases where the channeler's information has been refuted by hard evidence. The danger comes about when people tend to overlook the wrong information and assume that anything correctly stated in some way overrides it. Not so. If both the incorrect and the correct information is supposedly from the same spiritual source, then the existence of any wrong information shows that the source is not a source for truth. Truth mixed with error is still error.

Professional magicians who know how to stage illusions, like "the great" Houdini and "the amazing" Randi, have exposed the fraudulent ways of spiritists and channelers. Some science-oriented groups have also tested spiritists and found them using props and gimmicks for sound effects.

There is another realm of thinking that we must consider. Not all of the communications of the spiritists and channelers are attributed to stage tricks, even though the apparitions have been found fraudulent. We must, then, explain the messages they claim to receive. Channelers often receive thousands of unrehearsed words in perfect paragraphs, structure and outline, which are dictated to a scribe. From where do we attribute these communications, if not to the demonic realm? (cf., Chandler, *Understanding*, pp. 69-71)

A careful reading of Deuteronomy 13:1-4 shows us that the false dreamer (and the trance-channeler) will sometimes say things that come true (verse 2). The test for truth is not that something said may actually occur, the test is whom do the dreamers and channelers follow and whom do they tell others to follow (verse 2). If they teach any other god than the God of Israel, then they were not sent by Him (verses 3,4).

A few chapters later, in Deuteronomy 18:20-22, we find another test. (We must remember that the original was one entire message, without the chapter and verse divisions.) This test says if any part of the dreamer or channeler's message fails to happen, then he is not from God. The existence of one error prohibits our association.

When we apply this test to the channelers of the New Age, they miserably fail the standards of truth set down in Deuteronomy. There is not one channeler who is 100 percent accurate. Not one channeler teaches the truth about God. By this we know they are not from God.

Clairaudience and Spirit-guides

The meaning of clairaudience is from the French, "clear hearing." Clairaudience, then, is an ability claimed by psychics who hear what is not heard by others. It might be noises, music or voices, but the claimed perception is as "real" as audible sounds.

Some clairaudient people say they receive the communications only when they enter an altered-state of consciousness, the first stages of sleep, meditation, or hypnotic regression. The inner-voice is said to be clearly distinguishable from personal thoughts.

In the New Age Movement this has been one of the ways for people to contact their "spirit-guide," who then makes regular contact and guides them through life. It often matches the voice of a departed loved one.

New Agers are forever pointing to the Bible to validate their experiences. Every biblical passage used by those in the occult, barring none, is out of context and is falsely applied to a world view other than scriptural. The dead are prohibited from communicating with those on earth. No teaching on this is clearer than what Jesus gave in Luke 16:19-31. Lazarus was in Abraham's bosom (paradise) and the rich man was in hades (torment). The rich man begged Abraham to permit Lazarus to go back to earth and tell his five brothers about the torments of hell (verses 27,28). The answer was emphatically no. The reason is they have Moses and the prophets to tell them the truth (verses 29,31). The Scriptures are sufficient for us to obey; we do not need the dead to guide us.

Clairaudience and spirit-guides are also at odds with Scripture in John 16:13. Christians are assured that the Holy Spirit will "guide you into all the truth." What He speaks will not be mystical esoteric rambling. He will only do what glorifies Jesus (John 16:14). We are driven again back to the Bible for our standard of truth.

Clairvoyance

This term is used in psychic phenomena to describe a person who sees things that are not seen in the natural sense. The word comes from the French for "clear seeing." Clairvoyance is used as an umbrella for other psychic experiences including seeing auras and visions, out-of-body experiences, dreams, ESP, precognition, psychometry, and "ghost hunting" as practiced by those who enter houses to look for spirits or ghosts.

The New Age Movement has popularized clairvoyant acts but prefers trendy terms like psychic, psi energy and sixth-sense. All of these clairvoyant practices attempt to do the same thing: see by the use of the mind.

These practices open the person up to hallucinations and demonic activity. Any person who tries to contact the spirit world becomes a welcomed guest in the demonic dominion. Isaiah 8:19 tells us not to seek after spiritists (those who see spirits), but to seek after God instead. There are true visions mentioned in the Bible (Joel 2:28), and some people have false visions (Isaiah 28:7). They differ in that one is from God and one is from the enemy of His kingdom. Jeremiah 14:14 shows us that when visions are connected with any form of divination, they are not from God. Those who have false visions speak from the imagination and futility of their hearts (Jeremiah 23:16).

Crystals

Crystals are spectacular results of the creative work of God. They are beautiful to behold and keep an observer busy admiring every angle and each refraction of light glistening through their naturally formed facets. When God placed the properties within a geode to crystalize in the midst of cooling volcanic lava, He intended it for beauty, not for veneration as an "energy source."

The New Age Movement has placed emphasis upon the "vibration properties" and "energy sources" of crystals, which has launched an unheard of boom in the crystal sales market. Superstitious mystics have connected powers to crystals since the Middle Ages, when they were used as good luck charms and to ward off evil spirits. Within the New Age Movement, crystals are used for healing. New Age proponents believe that crystals can correct the universal life force within the human body, Ch'i (pronounced *key*), which is a product of the yang and yin forces. Or if one takes the Hindu approach, crystals are placed upon the chakras to harmonize the prana. In either method, practitioners believe the energy of the crystal can energize the ill human body.

Some New Agers use crystals for meditation, to strengthen creativity, release stress, enhance visualization or heighten psi perception. The supposed properties of crystals are explained in one New Age book as "very good transducers, amplifiers and focusing devices of the types of energies that affect our body sensors" (Milewski Harford, *The Crystal Sourcebook*, Sedona, AZ: Mystic Crystal Publications, 1988, p. xi).

The modern powers associated with crystals in New Age circles are rooted in the channeling of Edgar Cayce. Throughout his years as a trance-channeler he spoke often about Atlantis. The mythological destruction of Atlantis, through the misuse of an enormous crystaline power, only multiplied interest in the power of crystals. Cayce taught that there is an innate power within crystals.

Another channeler, Frank Alper, picked up on the Atlantis theme. He expanded the theory of crystalline power and published his collection of readings as *Exploring Atlantis*. These volumes, although not the only source on crystals, are major contributors to New Age beliefs. Alper taught that the innate power of a crystal is somehow stored, similar to a the power of a battery.

Scientifically, crystals can transform energy from an external source, as in a quartz watch or quartz radio. This is not what New Agers claim. They have an unscientific and unproven view that power exists within the crystal; furthermore, it can be transferred to human beings.

Crystals have no power or internal energy. They store nothing. They transfer nothing to humans. They cannot be drained and recharged like a battery, since they are not a power source. The metaphysical literature on crystals, published by New Age writers, is a deception and distortion of easily obtainable facts. Consulting any encyclopedia will set the record straight.

Lucifer is described in Ezekiel 28:13 as having every precious stone for his covering before he rebelled against God. He fell and lost his beauty. Now he has deceived New Agers into believing that the beauty of stones have power over their lives.

ESP and Parapsychology

The following of psychics in the New Age Movement is partly due to their methods of proselytizing. Whether they are in a television interview or writing a book, their message is the same, they preach that psychic abilities are in all of us and we only need to awaken them. "Just try it," they preach. "It is all natural," they say. We will compare what the gurus of the New Age are teaching with what the Bible says.

Parapsychology, a term coined by Emile Boirac (1857-1917), is a new branch of either the occult or psychology, depending on whom you consult. It is a discipline that has aimed to put many of the supernatural phenomena associated with the occult on sound scientific footing. The attempt is to create respectability for what has been considered as foolishness.

The occultic arts studied in parapsychology are usually those that are supposed to be latent powers within man, psychic powers. The popular designation for these powers is the twenty-third letter of the Greek alphabet—psi. Psi energy and psi powers are also known as extrasensory perception (ESP) or a sixth sense. The branches of psi studied in parapsychology are:

1. Clairvoyance (seeing in the past, present and future)

2. Precognition (knowing things in advance)

3. Psychokinesis (moving objects with mental power)

4. Telekineses (moving distant objects with mental power)

5. Telepathy (direct communication from one mind to another)

The scientific research on parapsychology in America was fathered by professors William Mc-Dougall and J. B. Rhine at Duke University (c. 1927). Two methods were used, employing a die and Zener cards. (Also known as ESP cards, a deck of twenty-five Zener cards has five sets of five symbols.)

Questions have been raised from the beginning about the control of these experiments. Parapsychologists promoted the Duke University studies as error-free proof of psychic power. To the parapsychologists' discredit, and later embarrassment, unconvinced researchers pointed out flaws in the loosely controlled experiments. When the controls were tightened on the same persons who had exhibited psi power, the results dropped dramatically. The new research disproved psi to the point that Rhine's subjects dropped to the level of chance guessing. Newer research into the records of Rhine, and other prominent psi studies (Soal), shows that some professors were willing to alter records and fabricate evidence to prove psi existed (cf., *Paranormal Phenomena*, Terry O'Neill, editor, San Diego: Greenhaven Press, Inc., 1990; and Thomas Gilovich, *How We Know What Isn't So*, New York: The Free Press, 1990, pp. 156-184).

In *Parapsychology and the Nature of Life,* John L. Randall comments on the way parapsychology surfaced for serious study:

> As the 1960s drew to a close parapsychology won a substantial victory in its ninety-year-old battle for scientific respectability. On December 30, 1969, the Parapsychological Association was officially accepted as an affiliate member of that most distinguished body of savants, the American Association for the Advancement of Science (A.A.A.S.). The decision to grant affiliation to the parapsychologists was taken by the A.A.A.S. council, an organization composed of delegates from about 300 other affiliated scientific, medical and engineering societies; so it represented the views of a considerable cross-section of American science. For the first time in its chequered history, parapsychology had been recognized as a legitimate scientific pursuit; and from now on parapsychologists could present their papers at the bar of scientific opinion without feeling that they would be ridiculed or dismissed out of hand merely on account of their subject matter (John L. Randall, *Parapsychology and the Nature of Life,* New York: Harper and Row Publishers, n.d., p. 175).

The demand for scientific investigation is a valid quest and should and must be made. This responsibility lies with Christians, too. However, in the consideration of parapsychology as science, one must be willing to embrace the most accurate explanation of the data, whether it be fraud, the occult or a valid paranormal experience.

In most cases, the study of parapsychology produces an increasing lack of motivation to study the Scriptures. In fact, it often leads one in the direction of the paranormal or supernatural totally apart from a biblical base.

Not only does this new emphasis on the science of parapsychology affect the way individuals understand

Christianity, it also affects the way people understand the Scriptures.

Scientists usually accept that similar phenomena occur in both the occult and parapsychology. However, many scientists disagree with the biblical explanation of such phenomena, that it is usually demonic. Often, the new science of parapsychology will discredit any biblical interpretation of the data.

For example, in the book, *Life, Death and Psychical Research: Studies on Behalf of the Churches' Fellowship for Psychical and Spiritual Studies*, the authors discredit the biblical admonition against sorcerers and mediums given in the Book of Deuteronomy. They feel this passage does not prohibit the exercise of psychical (demonic) gifts, the prohibition of which has been the historic and traditional interpretation by the church until the modern attempt to give some type, any type, of biblical credibility to the paranormal.

Consider this:

The Deuteronomic "prohibition" (Deuteronomy 18:9-12) has long been used by the prejudiced, the ignorant and the fearful as a reason for opposing genuine psychical research by Christian people. In the past, innocent folk have been denounced as sorcerers and witches or of being possessed by evil spirits. Others, who have exercised powers believed to come under the sacred ban, have been tortured to death.

Such attitudes still persist. Those who seek to exercise psychical gifts are often warned of the dangers of divine condemnation. Christians who encourage paranormal investigation are reminded that they are going against the teachings of the Bible and are forbidden to "dabble" in such matters (*Life Death and Psychical Research: Studies of the Churches' Fellowship for Psychical and Spiritual Studies*, Canon J.D. Pearce, Higgens and Rev. Stanley Whitby, eds., London: Rider and Company, 1973, p. 10).

While it's true innocent people have been denounced in the past (e.g., Salem witch trials), it is a logical fallacy to assume that historical interpretation of the Scriptures by Christians on this passage has been wrong. In fact, both history and proper biblical interpretation support Christianity's historical position.

Perception or Deception?

Most of the problem in scholastic tests of parapsychology is the lack of controlled experiments. This accounts for the high success rate of early studies at Duke University. The later controlled studies shed less than favorable light upon the former.

There are also a few showmen we will examine who deceived the public (and perhaps themselves) by claiming psychic powers when they were really using staged tricks. Their charade was exposed through investigative journalism and professional magicians/illusionists who revealed the secrets of the stunts.

One way an experiment can deceive the intelligent is to conduct the experiment in a poorly controlled atmosphere. Double-blind experiment conditions are better, but not fail-proof.

When we are dealing with the paranormal, there are several magician tricks that can be used by the participant for the appearance of psi abilities (cf., Danny Korem and Paul Meier, *The Fakers*, Grand Rapids, MI: Baker Book House, 1980, p. 107). If you take away the props, then the results of the experiment change. As an example, Dr. Rhine's most successful psychic was Hubert E. Pearce, Jr.. His name has become a mainstay among believers of psi ability. Upon further investigation it was found that he was allowed to shuffle the deck of cards himself before he guessed their order. Any magician can do the same! When this was brought to light, Dr. Rhine then had an assistant shuffle the cards. The experiment flopped—Pearce somehow lost his psi ability when he lost rights to the cards. When the prop is removed, the results change.

One study that shows the way controlled experiments are done:

> In these experiments a total of 66 subjects were tested. The number of card guesses involved 97,000. The technique generally used the screened touch-matching with modifications.
>
> There were two main series of experiments. In the longer B series the results of over 60,000 guesses produced a relatively low critical ratio of 4.99. Series A, which were conducted under less well-controlled conditions, showed a corresponding high ratio of 6.28, which is precisely what might be expected if the scoring successes were due solely to the intervention of sensory cues (D. H. Rawcliffe, *Illusions and Delusions of the Supernatural and the Occult*, New York: Dover Books, 1959, pp. 387-388).

What this study demonstrates is presence of ESP when the research is sloppy, and the lack of ESP when the research is controlled. This brings both the participants and experimenters under obligation to disclose precisely how each study was conducted before it can begin to be accepted. Even worse is J. B. Rhine's reluctant admission that he knew of fraud in the experiment! Martin Gardner comments upon the dishonesty:

> Turning to deliberate deception by parapsychologists, Rhine selects twelve sample cases of dishonest experimenters that came to his attention from 1940 to 1950, four of whom were caught "red-handed." Not a single name is mentioned. What papers did they publish, one wonders. Are their papers still being cited as evidence for psi? Rhine is convinced that such fraud diminished markedly after 1960. "We have at least got

past the older phase of having to use detectives and magicians to discover and prevent trickery by the subjects." He applauds the growing use of computers; but although "machines will not lie," he warns against overoptimism about their future usefulness in parapsychology. Complex apparatus, he cautions, "can sometimes also be used as a screen to conceal the trickery it was intended to prevent."

The warning proved prophetic. A few months after Rhine's paper appeared, the acting director of his laboratory and the young man he had chosen to be his successor, Dr. Walter Levy, was caught red-handed tinkering with an electronic recording machine. The tinkering had beefed up the scores of a test he was making on the PK [psychokinesis] ability of rats. Levy resigned in disgrace, though, again, references to his earlier papers (one on the PK powers of live chicken eggs) have not yet entirely vanished from psi literature. Rhine tried his best to hush up the scandal; but when it was obvious he could not do so, he wrote an apologetic article about it in his journal. As usual he did not mention Levy's name, apparently under the naive delusion that readers would not learn the flimflammer's identity.

Four years later, England's most distinguished parapsychologist, S. G. Soal, was caught having deliberately fudged the data for one of his most famous tests. I see no sign that Soal's other experiments are disappearing from the literature.

I have been told on reliable authority that the files in Rhine's laboratory contain material suggesting fraud on the part of Hubert Pearce, the most talented of all Rhine's early psychics. Who knows how much data of this sort is buried in the Rhine archives? Let us hope that someday someone with a balanced sense of history, under no compulsion to regard Rhine as one of psi's saints, will be allowed full access to those archives and give us a biography of Banks that is not a hagiography (*The Hundredth Monkey*, Centric Frazier, ed., Buffalo, NY: Prometheus Books, 1991, pp. 168-169).

Famous Psi Cases

Adam J. Linzmayer—Mr. Linzmayer was one of J. B. Rhine's first "successful" psychics. Discovered on the campus of Duke University, when Dr. Rhine opened his experiments in 1931, Linzmayer guessed the first nine Zener cards correctly. He hit 119 cards correctly out of 300 tries, which is twice the number from mere chance.

Was Linzmayer using psychic abilities? Some still believe so. However, the longer Dr. Rhine worked with Linzmayer the less psychic abilities he manifested. At the end of 2 years, his guesses were equal to chance (cf., *Psychic Powers*, Alexandria, VA: Time-Life Books, 1987, p. 52).

Hubert E. Pearce, Jr.—Pearce has been written of time and time again in parapsychology articles, journals and books. He was discovered in 1932, again, at Duke University. His claim to fame was a supposed perfect run of guessing all twenty-five Zener cards correctly. The odds are 1 in 298,023,223,876,953,125.

It seems that Pearce could gain psychic power when money was at stake. When he was first tested he could only guess ten of the twenty-five cards correctly. When Dr. Rhine offered Pearce $100 for each card guessed correctly, he hit a perfect score! Dr. Rhine was out $2,500 and Pearce was famous.

A flaw was discovered in the experiments at a later time. Pearce, it seems, felt better when he was allowed to shuffle the cards. One critic devised twenty ways Pearce could have cheated, including thumbnail marks, slight-of-hand, imperfections on the card backs (which were later mentioned), translucent card backs (which were later discovered), etc.

This problem was solved by placing Pearce in a room 100 yards away, from where he still hit thirteen of twenty-five cards correctly. This is better than the law of averages, but far below his success at $100 per card. A skeptical Duke University professor, C. M. Hansel, examined the room that was 100 yards away, and still found a way that cheating could have been involved, since both rooms were in the same building. Like Linzmayer before him, he eventually could not raise his guesses above the level of mere chance (ibid., p. 53; cf., Martin Gardner, *New Age Notes*, Buffalo, NY: Prometheus Books, 1991, p. 31).

Uri Geller—This man promoted himself as a psychic, with special abilities in psychokinesis (PK). He amazed audiences worldwide in person and on television as he appeared to bend keys, spoons, forks and other objects through mental powers. That is, until he was exposed as a fraud by James Randi. One of Geller's trick props was a large belt-buckle that secretly became a bending device when he distracted the audience.

Another of Geller's tricks was revealed by illusionist Henry Gordon. Geller had a mental telepathy stunt where he would choose a person from the audience, turn his back to a chalkboard (while facing the audience) and ask the person to write a word on the board. People were amazed at his apparent ability to read minds and know the correct word. What they did not know was that Geller had a confidant who was sitting in the front row, signaling letters of the alphabet to him.

The public exposure of Geller's fraud caused an end to his career. It seems that his psychic ability ended too.

The Amazing Kreskin—George Kreskin is another showman who crossed over the line of truth by claiming he had psi powers. Fellow magicians became troubled when this happened, so they exposed him as a fraud.

Professional illusionist Henry Gordon says:

> [Kreskin] has not yet done anything I cannot dupli-
> cate . . . Most of his effects are standard commercial tricks
> found in the magic market . . . I part company with Kres-
> kin when he implies that he has special powers of ESP
> (*ExtraSensory Deception*, Buffalo, NY: Prometheus, 1987,
> p. 25).

Does a Sixth Sense Exist?

How should one evaluate paranormal experiences? One must admit the possibility that such
experiences may occur. Dr. J. B. Rhine of Duke
University's Parapsychology Laboratory spent a
lifetime in an attempt to document the reality of extra-
sensory perception.

It can be said that if there is some type of ESP
capacity within some individuals, independent of either
divine or demonic influence, its moral value would
depend on its use. However, there seems to be an un-
likelihood of divine use or aid.

The Scriptures have strong language about the use
of such powers, where their use is referred to as not
being of God. The major emphasis of such ESP experience, as has been shown, generally does not lead
one toward biblical truth.

Lynn Walker sums up the present situation well as
he points out that today almost all forms of paranormal
activity have no relation to the God of the Bible.

> We must conclude that it is when man, through the
> influence of Satan's direct power, uses a God-given talent
> or ability to teach religious error (Colossians 2:8-10; 2
> Corinthians 11:3,4), to promote works of the flesh
> (Galatians 5:19), to exalt self as specially endowed by
> God as his agent (Colossians 2:18; 2 Corinthians 10:18), to
> deny the God of the Bible (2 Peter 2:1), to deliberately
> aspire to go beyond bounds divinely set (Deuteronomy

29:29)—it is then that man has become an instrument of Satan, a tool of evil supernaturalism. Divination in its multiplied forms and all present-day claims to revelations from God are equally Satan-inspired (Lynn Walker, *Supernatural Power and the Occult*, Austin, TX: Firm Foundation Publishing House, n.d., p. 91).

Fire Walking

Fire walking is an ancient practice of someone walking barefoot across a fiery bed of coals or stones without the slightest pain or any damage to the person. It is still widely practiced in Japan, India and the Fiji Islands.

Since some magicians can duplicate fire walking by trickery, some people dismiss all fire walking as trickery. The trick is accomplished by relying upon short contact with the hot stones, which prevents the walker from being burned.

Danny Korem comments:

It has been found that one cannot take more than four steps across a bed of coals without running the risk of being burned. In 1937, Ahmed Hussain, another coal walker, took six steps in 2.3 seconds to cross a twenty-foot pit (temperature 740 degrees Celsius) and was severely burned. There have been other laymen, however, who have successfully duplicated the coal-walking stunt.

Walking on heated stones is even easier, since stone is a poor conductor of heat. You will not, however, witness a fakir walk across a heated steel plate, as steel is an excellent conductor of heat (Danny Korem and Paul Meier, *The Fakers*, Grand Rapids, MI: Baker Book House, 1980, p. 89).

There are others who see fire walking not as a magician's trick but rather as an occultic practice. This is the position of Kurt Koch, who writes:

In Japan a former fire walker came to me to be counseled. He confessed to his former activities and said that he had really deceived the audience. The fire had been made on a high platform down the center of which had been a narrow path. Either side of this path was a fire of wood coals. The people around and below the platform had not been able to see the path through the fire. I asked this man if he thought all fire walking was faked in the same way. He replied, "No. Most of it is genuine. It is only faked sometimes for the sake of the tourists."

In South Africa another fire walker confessed to his occult practice. The man was an Indian who worked on a sugar plantation. He told me that he could really walk through fire. He would prepare himself for some days through fasting and meditation, abstaining from alcohol and sexual intercourse, eating only a vegetarian diet, etc. I asked him if he thought the powers he possessed over fire originated from his own subconscious mind. "That's impossible," he replied. "The devil gives this power to those who serve him." He went on to confess that when he had become a Christian he had lost his power to walk through fire.

I know that hypnosis and trance states can protect fire walkers from the pain, but they cannot protect a person from being burnt. One day in India a young mother walked through fire with her small baby. However, she was not fully prepared for the ordeal. Her baby fell from her arms into the fire and was dead within a few seconds. Before the people could reach it, its body was burned to ashes.

Behind the phenomenon of genuine fire walking there are demonic forces at work, and newly born Christians can feel this in the atmosphere (Kurt Koch, *The Devil's Alphabet*, Grand Rapids, MI: Kregel Publications, n.d., pp. 54,55).

Is there fire walking in the Bible? The Bible gives an account (Daniel 3:21-29) of three men of God who were supernaturally protected when they were thrown into a burning furnace. The God of the Bible protected them because they were being punished for refusing to worship false gods. There are some who try to say this is an example of and justification of fire walking. By reading the account in Daniel, you can see that there is no parallel. The three men of God were preserved to bring glory and honor to the true God, not to amuse on-lookers or make the performers rich. One who points to Daniel 3 as justification of fire walking makes a mock-ery of God's Word.

In conclusion it seems difficult to place all cases of fire walking in the category of trickery or self-hypnosis. But whatever the case may be, fire walking is an ungod-ly ritual attempting to get the eyes of the observers away from the true and living God. Some see this prac-tice as Satan's imitation of God's miracle in delivering the three Jews from the fiery furnace, showing that the devil has equal power. This, as we have seen, is not the case.

Holistic Health

The New Age Movement ushered in a number of new words for our growing vocabulary. Holistic, holism, and bioenergy are among the few pertaining to this subject. Holism is the belief that the human body has a universal life-force called Ch'i or prana (Hin-duism). The life force (called bioenergy in the New Age Movement) must be balanced in order for the body, mind and spirit to function at their peak performance. Holistic is the way to bring the body back into its har-mony with the universal life force. It treats all three aspects simultaneously by raising consciousness, heightening emotions and balancing Ch'i.

The holistic health movement has opened our eyes to the toxins, chemicals, pollutants and bad qualities of processed food. In this they may have been a catalyst in public awareness (although they were not the first—the Seventh-day Adventists were on the cutting edge of warning America about unhealthy food decades ago).

There is nothing inherently wrong with watching what you eat, and it is advisable to read product labels, take vitamins and cut back on high cholesterol diets. This is also a commendable by-product of the health consciousness movement.

The New Age effect takes place when one believes that eating certain foods, popping mega-doses of vitamins, meditating for mind-balance, visualizing the perfect you, practicing yoga for proper Ch'i flow, and entertaining a host of other New Age techniques will produce unity of the mind, body and spirit. This is the crossover from health consciousness to spiritual deception. The most dangerous deception occurs when a person becomes ill and the New Age diagnosis is more clairvoyant than scientific. Iridology is one such example; it claims to diagnose organic illness from an examination of the iris. These techniques are based upon unscientific methods, have dubious results and hold an unbiblical world view.

Homeopathy

Even though homeopathy (Greek: *homois,* "similar," "pathos," "suffering") did not originate in the New Age Movement, it has been promoted as a natural and holistic way of health. It is neither, and it certainly should be examined since it has the occultic origin of psychic diagnosis and treatment. There is nothing scientific about it. We have found Christians who testify of its healing power, until we have shown them the ingredients, that are at best a placebo, and at worse a doorway to misdiagnosis of real problems. The greatest danger is spiritual for those who believe in the occultic teaching of homeopathy.

Homeopathy began with a German physician, Samuel Christian Hahnemann (1755-1843), who studied mesmerism directly under Franz A. Mesmer in Vienna. Mesmerism (often equated with hypnosis) originally held the belief that the body has a magnetic energy field. Dr. Mesmer would place jars containing "magnetized" water in a large tub. Protruding from the stopper at the neck of the jar was an iron rod, half above the stopper and half submerged in the water below it. Dr. Mesmer would have his patients sit close to the tub, holding hands, to begin the flow of "animal magnetism" in their bodies. At the given time they were told to grab one of the iron rods (for more magnetism) and touch the ailing part of their body with the other hand. The patients would experience convulsions, hysteria, laughter, crying and an array of outbursts until calmed by the wave of Dr. Mesmer's hand or a snap of his fingers (hence, the connection to hypnosis).

Dr. Hahnemann accepted this theory and wrote of its successes in his first book *Organon of Rational Healing* (1810). It is through this book that he also advanced his theory for homeopathy.

"Homeopathy," he said, " . . . can easily convince every reflecting person that the diseases of man are not caused by any substance, and acridity, that is to say any disease matter, but that they are solely spirit-like (dynamic), derangements of the spirit-like power (the vital principle), that animates the human body."

His animal magnetism was advanced in the same work:

It acts in part homeopathically by exciting symptoms similar to those of the disease to be cured, and is applied for this purpose by a single pass or stroke of the hands held flatwise over the body, and carried, during moderate exertions of the will, from the crown to the tips of the toes, this process is efficacious in uterine hemorrhages, even when death is imminent (cited by Martin Gardner, *Fads and Fallacies in the Name of Science*, New York: Dover Books, 1959, p. 336).

Dr. Hahnemann saw animal magnetism and homeopathy as one essence. Both theories hold that the body has a vital life force, that diseases are spiritually induced and spiritually cured. This indisputable fact about the true source of homeopathy has been silently swept under the rug of the homeopathic practitioner.

Embarrassed by homeopathy's occultic origin, most practitioners say that Dr. Hahnemann discovered homeopathy when he digested Peruvian bark (a source of quinine) and produced similar symptoms as malaria—discomfort, fever and chills. He theorized that a substance (Peruvian bark) that causes similar symptoms (pseudo-malaria) in a healthy person, would then cure the real symptoms (real malaria) in an ill person. This "law of similia" states that all diseases are cured by a substance that produces a similar symptom of the real disease. (If a substance produces the symptoms of a migraine headache in a healthy person, then giving that substance to a sufferer of migraine headaches will cure him.) In contrast, critics believe that Hahnemann was actually allergic to quinine and manifested an allergic reaction rather than symptoms of malaria (cf, Samuel Pfeiffer, M. D., *Healing at Any Price*, England: Word Limited, 1988, p. 65).

Hahnemann's non-germ theory of disease, that all disease is spiritual in its cause, led him to the parallel belief of spiritual cure. The way this works is by giving the patient the least amount he can handle of homeopathic medicine. The diluted amounts are referred to in Roman numerals for ten (X) and one hundred (C).

Health food stores are the largest outlet of homeopathic remedies, which are available in two forms, liquid and tablet. The liquid remedy contains one part substance with ten parts water or alcohol. This combination is called "1X" on the bottle, meaning 1/10 per volume. The liquid is vigorously shaken for homogenization. Then it can be used for the more potent cut by extracting 1/10 of the 1X to form 1/100 or 2X, cut it again to make 1/1000 or 3X, etc. By the time the combination is called 6X, it is 1/1,000,000 of the original. Powerful stuff! Homeopaths believe that, instead of getting weaker when cut, the remedy gets stronger through spiritual power. The homeopathic theory is that the least amount is the most potent. Homeopaths are known to cut the combination to one decillionth (a millionth of a millionth, of a millionth, of a millionth, of a millionth, of a millionth, of a millionth, of a millionth, of a millionth, of a millionth). This is so infinitesimal, we wonder if the person isn't better off with nothing.

The tablet form is made in the same way, except it begins with 9/10 milk sugar (lactose) and 1/10 substance. Those who want the best mixture begin with 1/100 substance and 99/100 lactose. The cutting process is labeled as 1C, 2C, 3C, etc., all the way down to a substance amount of one molecule. How does homeopathy explain the value of one molecule of substance? This is where the spiritual power significantly comes into play, homeopaths believe. One molecule of the original substance in the pill or liquid (12C or 24X) releases a great amount of power because of its small size. This power is transferred from the molecule to the remaining volume during the vigorous shaking. The little molecule's great spiritual essence affects the entire batch, which is why it is so potent.

We keep speaking of homeopathic substance but we have not said what that substance is. More than 3,000 remedies are made from herbs, powdered starfish, skunk secretion, crushed live bed bugs, powdered coal, powdered shells, human urine, and snake excrement, to name a few (Gardner, op. cit., p. 189). The March 1952 issue of *The Journal of the American Institute of Homeopathy* (Philadelphia, PA) gave remedies using spider poison and spider webs. All these ingredients bring to mind a witch's brew from an old black and white movie. And speaking of ingredients brings up another problem with homeopathy—the bottle labels do not tell you what the ingredients are. It doesn't matter, however, because the spiritual power generated heals, homeopaths say.

Homeopathy begins with the occult and ends with it. New Agers have embraced it because it fits their world view of man and bioenergy. Christians need to be aware that it is founded upon false and unbiblical principles and leads its adherents into deception.

Crossover Practices

A few practices that have a legitimate basis have been crossing over into New Age holism. Christian doctors use these practices without any compromise of their Christian beliefs, but the same within the hands of a New Age practitioner have an unbiblical metaphysical overtone.

Herbology

That God created herbs for our health is undeniable in Scripture (Genesis 1:29). Herbs have been used as a basis for medicine from the earliest of times. Also undeniable is the value of herbs as digestive aids and the like. There has been a notable return to looking at herbs and natural substances for medicinal purposes. With herbs we do not quarrel because we are using what God created for legitimate purposes.

The crossover of herbology into the New Age occurs when herbs are seen as possessing powers exaggerated beyond the natural realm and into the metaphysical. The New Age Movement attaches powers to herbs to bring the body back into its bioenergetic harmony. One source for this teaching has been Chinese herbology. This source can be unhealthy, since it has not been tested, and it is unbiblical because it is based on the Taoist world view.

Biofeedback and Pain Control

This modern method of attaching sensors to the body to register voluntary control of pain or to lower blood pressure has no innate problem. If God has given us the ability to live with pain, then the biofeedback machine is incidental to it. Many people have learned pain control without its use.

It is not until this machine is in the hands of a New Ager that it becomes an issue. At that point, it shifts from a pain control device to a Ch'i harmonizing device and becomes a method for entering New Age holism. Use of the machine is then usually accompanied by meditation or bioenergy teachings.

Hypnosis

Hypnosis is an altered state of consciousness that may be induced through a number of methods. The three main states are light, medium and deep hypnosis. The light state (lethargic) ranges from self-induction of auto-suggestion to spontaneous hypnosis. The medium state (cataleptic) is induced through a second party, but the subject remains responsive. This is commonly used for mild dental work to reduce fear in a patient. In this state a person may come out of the hypnosis by himself. The deep, trance-like state (somnambulistic) is induced by a second party and places the subject in a sleep-like state. This is often used in stage shows, non-anesthetic medical care, psychology, and occult practices.

Encyclopedia Britannica defines hypnosis as:

A sleeplike state that nevertheless permits a wide range of behavioral responses to stimulation. The hypnotized individual appears to heed only the communications of the hypnotist ... Even memory and awareness of self may be altered by suggestion, and the effects of the suggestions may be extended (post-hypnotically) into subsequent waking activity (*Encyclopedia Britannica*, Chicago: Encyclopedia Britannica Publishers, 1974, Macropaedia, Volume 9, p. 133).

The light state of hypnosis is usually self-induced through auto-suggestion or another means. Weight control and smoking control programs are popular ways self-hypnosis is used. Another way light hypnosis happens is through viewing the repetitious white lane dividers on road surfaces, particularly in night driving, when the headlights accentuate the white lines in the vision of the driver. This spontaneous phenomenon is commonly called "road hypnotism" and is recognized when the driver's attention lapses.

These examples belong to the light state of hypnotism. However, the light hypnotic state can be used wrongly, resulting in a bad spiritual effect.

The self-hypnosis cassette tapes that are so popular in the New Age Movement cannot be justified for use by Christians because they do not know the world view of the person producing the tape. New Age teachings are often subtly slipped into the tape here and there. Even if the light state of hypnosis is self-induced, or spontaneous for that matter, it does not mean people should actively pursue it.

The Bible instructs us to think. Philippians 4:8,9 gives us eight suggestions of things to think upon. If you, as a Christian, feel the need to think on things repeatedly—in an auto-suggestion manner—we cannot say with certainty it is harmful. However, there is nothing you can do through auto-suggestion that cannot be done through prayer and a disciplined life.

The other two states of hypnotism are used in a variety of ways. Some occult oriented religionists practice extreme methods of self-hypnosis in an attempt to make themselves insensitive to the pain of sticking sharp instruments through various parts of their body. Some magicians use hypnosis as a means of entertaining the public. It is not unusual for schools to allow magic shows where the magician will call up several students in order to hypnotize them.

Many physicians use hypnosis for diagnosis and therapy in treating illnesses. The idea is to alter negative aspects of a person's behavior. Another use of hypnotism, which is much too common, is the occult practice of one who uses hypnotism as a magic art to control the behavior of individuals, or for past-life regression.

There is a wide difference of opinion on the validity and usefulness of hypnotism. Some see hypnotism as being neutral, neither good nor bad, while psychologists argue that hypnotism can be beneficial for diagnosis and therapy. There are yet others who see hypnotism as harmful, no matter what the case, because it is an attack on the human psyche.

Christian counselor Kurt Koch gives many examples of hypnosis which have ended in disaster. We would strongly warn people to stay away from all forms of either occultic or entertaining hypnosis (cf., *Between Christ and Satan*, Grand Rapids: Kregal Publications, 1979, p. 65*f.*).

Is There Any Positive Use for Hypnosis?

Hypnotism has been practiced on missionary fields for medical reasons, especially in the absence of anesthesia. The same has been true during wartime.

What can we say about these situations? Is there any justification for the use of hypnosis during such times?

A physician is not interested in influencing a person's subconscious mind during a medical emergency. Physicians who have to use hypnosis in place of anesthesia use it for one purpose: so the person will feel no pain. If a person allows himself to be hypnotized, it should be only under the most controlled situation by a qualified and experienced physician. The human mind is not something to play with or to let another person have control of. At best, hypnosis can have only limited use.

It has been shown that a person in the deep-state of hypnosis cannot be made to do something against his will. Nevertheless, there is an obvious spiritual danger in allowing a psychologist, occultist, stage magician, or an unknown party to speak to the subconscious mind.

In the hands of an occultist or New Ager the purpose of hypnosis is usually for recalling past lives (reincarnation), remembering one's birth, or contacting a spirit-guide. A therapist may use hypnosis for crime investigation, UFO abduction recall, Satanic ritual abuse recall, multiple personality investigation, or some form of therapy. These are all spiritually dangerous because they release the mind to fantasize uncontrolled by reason.

Hypnosis can be a very dangerous thing that destroys lives rather than repairs them. The devil's playground is full of toys, but the games end up destroying lives. Jesus said the devil came to steal, kill and destroy (John 10:10).

New Age Meditation

Meditation is defined as the act of contemplation. In the New Age Movement it becomes just about every-

thing except contemplation. As a matter of fact, meditation in New Age groups carries the idea of a
non-thinking state, stilling the activity of the mind,
losing oneself in the bliss of silence, or releasing oneself
from conscious thinking.

New Age meditation is occultic and is dependent
upon monism (all is one) or pantheism (all is God) for
its world view. Its goal is to become one with the One
through meditation. Achieving this goal may take place
through meditating on a mantra (often the name of a
Hindu god), or focusing on an object, like a candle.
Sometimes certain postures are prescribed to help energy flow during meditation (yoga). The bliss which
occurs is an occultic spiritual deception produced after
one puts aside the "illusion" of this world and recognizes his own internal "divine" nature, i.e., his oneness
with the universal god of which the meditater believes
he is a spark.

The belief that man can be like God is what caused
sin to enter the world (Genesis 3). Biblical meditation
emphasizes just the opposite, that man is the creature
and God is the Creator. Biblical meditation also involves
thinking. Psalm 1:2,3 tells us to meditate (think) upon
the law of the Lord. By thinking upon Him, His at-
tributes, His Word, we deepen our appreciation for His
grace and salvation. Christian meditation must always
be focused upon biblical truths, seeing God as the in-
finitely wise Creator and man as a fallen race
dependent upon his grace. Christian meditation always
humbles one's soul rather than elevating it to the
Divine (Philippians 2:1-5).

Out-of-Body and Near-Death Experiences

Astral projection is the old term, used by the
Theosophical Society, for out-of-body experiences
(OBE). The Astral plain was what Madame Balvatski

called the spirit world, so Astral projection became the term used for soul-travel in the spirit world. Although others had claimed the experience of soul-travel before Madame Balvatski's time, Theosophy became the springboard for research, study and interest for the twentieth century.

An OBE is the popular description given to soul-travel in the New Age Movement. The OBE is divided into two categories for study: voluntary and involuntary.

Voluntary OBE happens when a person willfully projects or dismisses his soul from the confines of his body and allows it to travel a distance. Voluntary OBE is practiced in some New Age groups and is written of by Shirley MacLaine, L. Ron Hubbard, Madame Balvatski, Robert Monroe and others.

Involuntary OBE is subdivided into two areas. The first type occurs in this way: a person subjected to preoperative anesthesia leaves his body and observes himself and others around him while he is lying on the bed or operating table. This OBE is called involuntary because the person does not actively pursue the experience and most often it is unexpected. Some people refer to this as spontaneous OBE, which has also taken place under hypnosis.

The second type of involuntary OBE became the subject of a specialized study called near-death experiences (NDE). This phenomenon always occurs involuntarily and spontaneously. It has the peculiar trait of occurring after one has been pronounced dead or perhaps during the resuscitation procedure of CPR, electro-shock, or a similar life-saving attempt.

There is still much more to investigate and understand about OBEs and NDEs. The voluntary OBE may be generally attributed to the occult, since most of the people who practice it are involved in the New Age Movement and/or occultism.

Involuntary OBEs and NDEs propose a problem because of their involuntary nature. Because of that trait, some theologians have openly embraced NDEs as viable proof of life after death. The criticisms of OBEs and NDEs from the scientific community are usually negative. However, when we examine the scientists' conclusions, we very often find them shallow and not true to the event, or they are hasty generalizations. Reading both sides of the issue, by qualified experts in *Paranormal Phenomena* (pp. 218-228), one gets the feeling that investigating scientists are grasping at straws and not trying to match the experiences with adequate explanations.

A more integral job of investigating by a scientist was done by Susan Blackmore in *Not Necessarily the New Age* (Robert Basil, ed., Buffalo, NY: Prometheus Books, 1988, pp. 165-184). She challenged the flimsy models advanced by Carl Sagon and others. She should be commended for her sensitivity to the facts, but she still appears to juggle theories to form her hypothesis.

Plainly, science does not have an explanation for OBEs and NDEs. Asking a series of "why" questions may be intellectually stimulating, but it disproves nothing. Two points worthy of consideration, though: (1) that hallucination and voluntary OBEs are similar, and (2) that OBE-like experiences can be produced by electrical stimulation of the temporal lobes of the brain (*The Hundredth Monkey*, pp. 48-50). The problem is that these OBE-like hallucinations and the experiences produced by stimulations do not fit the entire description of the OBE. It is a fallacy of logic to say that similarity shows the same origin.

Our attempt here will be to work toward an answer that fits the experience and that stays within the guidelines of Scripture. While scientists try to look at cause and ignore the content, we would like to theologically examine the content, which then may partially explain the origin or at least some of the causes.

In comparison of voluntary OBEs and drug hallucinations, we must note that neither can describe what is outside of his body in true detail. The scientists who conducted brain-stimulation (quite some time ago in Canada) found the OBE description of the room was not true in detail. This leads us to questions about truth and where the false information comes from. Two accounts, from men who have had over 2,000 OBEs, will serve to illustrate the false information. One is often a child and the other is often female in the OBEs. The latter also claims to have entered a corpse when trying to return to his body (cf., *Harpers*, pp. 421-423). This does not mean that all voluntary OBEs are demonically inspired, but it certainly says that although the experience was "real," it was not true.

Looking at the involuntary OBEs and NDEs presents a different problem, since some people who have experienced these had strong Christian testimonies beforehand and some who were not Christians before their experience became so afterward. We need to exercise a word of caution here. It is far too great an error to give the involuntary OBE and NDE a clean bill of health without a thorough checkup. There are also many people who have had involuntary OBEs and NDEs who went into the occult, so the experience does not necessarily lead one to Christ (cf., John Weldon and Clifford Wilson, *Occult Shock and Psychic Forces*, San Diego: Master Books, 1980, p. 95).

Even though reports have been given in NDEs that "Christ" was at the end of the tunnel, not every report agreed on this point. Some said it was light, love or Buddha at the end of their tunnel. This could give people the false impression that whatever one believes is perfectly fine and produces the same end result. Nothing could be further from the teachings of Jesus. He singled himself out as the only way to heaven (Matthew 24:3-5; John 10:1-8; 14:6). The fact that some people become Christians through NDEs is incidental to the question of whether it is truth. Who can count the number of people who have turned away from Christ because of NDEs endorsing false religions?

The apostle Paul admonished those at Thessalonica to reject things that are false (1 Thessalonians 5:21) and we should too. Since most people who have voluntary OBEs are into the occult, we cannot rule out the strong possibility that their OBEs are demonic-inspired visions leading them after another god (Deuteronomy 18:10-12).

Experience is not our guide for interpreting Scripture, viz., we experience it; therefore it must be true. No, to the contrary. Scripture is our guide for experience. We have an experience; now let's test it by Scripture! The apostle John evidently knew Christians who had experiences that needed to be tested too: "Beloved, do not believe every spirit, but test the spirits to see whether they are from God; because many false prophets have gone out into the world" (1 John 4:1).

Psychokinesis (PK) and Telekinesis

These two words, although somewhat synonymous, have this distinction: psychokinesis is the attempt to move an object though mental power; telekineses is the attempt to move a distant object through mental power. Distance is the distinction.

The Israeli mentalist Uri Geller gained international attention for his psychokinetics. He claimed psi powers could bend keys, spoons, forks, and other objects. To his dismay, he was proven a fraud. There has never been a legitimate case of psychokinetics or telekinetics yet. Some form of magician's trick has always been used.

The New Age danger is that thousands of people still believe Uri Geller has psi powers. Some books still speak of his abilities as if they were genuine.

We do not want to throw out the possibility that some who claim psychokinesis power may be working in conjunction with demonic powers. Uri Geller, explained to his loyal fans that he sometimes used props because he had no control over his psi powers and he did not know when they would work. This is a clever way to get out of being caught with props. Any time he is caught, then he merely says the prop was a back up. When he is not caught, then he claims to have real psi powers.

Pyramid Power

Pyramid power exploded onto the scene in the 1970s due to some experiments with a Czech radio engineer who discovered that a miniature pyramid will keep razor blades sharp for weeks on end. It was not as if the little double-edged throw-away blades of that era were scarce, but the focus was how did pyramids effect them and keep them sharp (up to fifty shaves). Czechoslovakian born Karel Drbal actually made the discovery in 1959. News of his discovery did not become popular in America until 1970.

The public interest turned faddish as pyramids were marketed in mass quantity and sizes. Newspapers, major magazines, and scientific publications all joined in reporting results of experiments where fruit and meat remained fresh without refrigeration. Electromagnetic microwaves became the most natural explanation for the sharp razor blades and non-decaying fruit. Tiny drops of moisture are drawn from edge of the blade which keeps the edge from dulling and corroding. (The same effect can be done with forced air or an alcohol rinse.) The fruit was actually in a slow process of dehydration.

To the New Ager, though, it is not natural but mystical. Pyramid power in the New Age was a way to enhance psi power. Large pyramids were hung above beds for energy, some New Agers wore pyramid hats during meditation, others used pyramids for healing.

Combining occultism and pyramids can result in spiritism. J. Z. Knight, a world-famous channeler who speaks for Ramtha (her spirit-guide from Atlantis), claims her first contact with Ramtha was via a pyramid hat. She held a pyramid on her head in 1978 and an entity appeared in her kitchen. She has channeled his messages for New Age followers since then.

Any object can be used as a tool for Satan. Let's look at a perplexing statement by the apostle Paul. He said, "an idol is nothing in itself," in 1 Corinthians 8:4. When we study how Satan and his minions use the idol then we can better understand how that applies to New Age objects. The idol by itself has no power, its power comes from the fallen spirits that work through it. The same is true for so many New Age objects. The object is nothing by itself, but when spirits work through it we see the diabolical scheme of Satan against mankind: It takes people away from looking to God.

Reincarnation

Reincarnation has been taught in various cultures around the world, but it has always been at odds with the people of God, both in the Old Testament and the New Testament.

One of the oldest of all religious beliefs is that of reincarnation. If one will closely study ancient religions, the teaching of reincarnation will appear frequently in a variety of forms. The belief in reincarnation, however, is not limited to ancient religions but is widely held today by many different religious, cultic and occultic groups, including the New Age Movement.

The idea behind reincarnation is that a person's soul lives a succession of lives which will eventually terminate when that person has, by his deeds, rid himself of all sin. This state where reincarnation is no longer necessary is known in Eastern thought as nirvana, or becoming one with the divine universe. The person is born, lives and dies and comes back with a new body (hence, reincarnation). The cycle usually continues until that person reaches eternal bliss.

The Western concept of reincarnation is not the same as the Eastern teaching of transmigration of the soul. Transmigration of the soul permits the person to return not only in human bodies but also in plants and animals.

While reincarnation is limited to the human body, "transmigration is still the teaching of pure Hinduism, but many offshoots of Hinduism and most Western proponents of such ideas have rejected transmigration and now embrace only reincarnation" (Walter Martin, *The New Cults*, p. 352).

Many people turn to the Bible in an attempt to support the idea of reincarnation, but a study of the Scripture will reveal that the Bible is diametrically opposed to reincarnation. Rather than teach that we can have many deaths and rebirths, the Bible makes it clear that there is only one death per person (Hebrews 9:27).

But what about the various cases of alleged reincarnation which have been publicized in recent years, some sounding very convincing? One answer to this lies in the spiritual warfare spoken of in Scripture. The Bible says that "we wrestle not with flesh and blood, but against principalities, against powers, against the rulers of the darkness of this world, against spiritual wickedness in high places" (Ephesians 6:12, KJV).

There is a spiritual battle going on, and if people can be convinced that there is no judgement after this life but merely a progression into the next, then they will feel no need to receive Jesus Christ as Savior. We believe it is one of the desires of Satan and his hosts to convince people they must atone for their own sins, and belief in reincarnation is one of these devices.

People experience what they believe is a regression into a past when in actuality their experience is in the realm of the occult. It is easy for demonic forces, which have been around from the beginning of the earth, to reveal to someone some alleged past act or experience. You will note that any so-called reincarnation experience always leads people away from the God of the Bible and the death of Christ on the cross for the forgiveness of sins.

The possibility of fraud also may be involved in so-called reincarnation experiences. The information brought out during the times of regression could be obtained by other means, such as some research about the person who supposedly is speaking. This type of fraud has been perpetrated with regard to spiritists who have "inside information" about the dead ones who allegedly speak during a seance. In reality the medium has done his homework and this can impress the participant with little-known information about the dead. The same type of thing happens in many supposed cases of reincarnation.

Reincarnation teaches that only through many lifetimes can one rid himself of the debt for all of his sins. However, the Bible teaches that through Jesus Christ we can be rid of the penalty for all our sins at one time (1 John 1:8-10). His purpose for dying on the cross was a sacrifice for our sins (Acts 3:18,19).

Jesus Christ is the only Savior we ever need because "He abides forever, holds His priesthood permanently. Hence, also, He is able to save forever those who draw near to God through Him, since He always lives to make intercession for them" (Hebrews 7:24,25). We have the promise of God Himself that our salvation has been guaranteed through faith in the sacrifice of Jesus Christ on the cross (1 Peter 1:2-6).

As Christians we look forward to resurrection, not reincarnation. Since the fall of man (Genesis 3) the entire universe has been abnormal. Man, animals, nature—all have been placed under the sentence of death. God said to Adam, "By the sweat of your face you shall eat bread, till you return to the ground, because from it you were taken; for you are dust, and to dust you shall return" (Genesis 3:19).

Mankind has always looked forward to something better, namely, a resurrection into a new body on a new planet Earth that has been renovated by God. The Scriptures speak of the time when we shall all be changed:

> Behold, I tell you a mystery; we shall not all sleep, but we shall all be changed, in a moment, in the twinkling of an eye, at the last trumpet; for the trumpet will sound, and the dead will be raised imperishable, and we shall be changed. For this perishable must put on the imperishable, and this mortal must put on immortality. But when this perishable will have put on the imperishable, and this mortal will have put on immortality, then will come about the saying that is written, "Death is swallowed up in victory. O death, where is your victory? O death, where is your sting?" The sting of death is sin, and the power of sin is the law; but thanks be to God, who gives us the victory through our Lord Jesus Christ (1 Corinthians 15:51-57).

Elsewhere the Scripture says we shall be made like

Him at the resurrection, "Beloved, now are we children of God, and it has not appeared as yet what we shall be. We know that, when He appears, we shall be like Him, because we shall see Him just as He is" (1 John 3:2).

Furthermore the whole creation will be made new:

> "And He shall wipe away every tear from their eyes; and there shall no longer be any death; there shall no longer be any mourning, or crying, or pain; the first things have passed away." And He who sits on the Throne said, "Behold, I am making all things new" (Revelation 21:4,5).

Thus, the Bible gives the believer the promise of a new body and a new world at the resurrection of the dead. This can be received by belief in Christ, not through a series of rebirths as taught by reincarnation.

Clifford Wilson and John Weldon show some of the differences between Christianity and reincarnation:

Christianity	Reincarnation
Believes in judgment that is eternal, following man's death.	States we have many lives , even thousands, to perfect ourselves.
Believes in the atonement for sins.	States we have no need for a savior, therefore denies the necessity of salvation; there is no need for it, according to the nature of "reality."
Believes in the deity of Christ.	Vague and contradictory views on "God." States there is no need for Jesus to be God—He was just more advanced ("He's been through more incarnations") than most.
Believes in the existence	All evil is a result of man's

of personal devil or Satan, and fallen evil spirits—demons.	choosing. Satan is devised by human institution. Evil spirits are held to be regressed human spirits between incarnations, not demons.
Believes in the Bible as God's only Word to mankind.	Opposes biblical concepts: e.g., Hebrews 9:27. All religious Scriptures or writings are communications from God or the spirit world to help man.
Believes in a personal God, revealed as the Trinity of Father, Son, and Holy Spirit.	Denies a personal triune God. Ultimate reality is often impersonal karmic law.
Believes in heaven as a distinct, eternal place.	Various progressive spirit-realms.
Believes in the sinlessness of Christ.	Denies it; no one is perfect (some may say Christ has now reached perfection, but that He was a sinner like everyone else, beforehand).
Believes in the physical eternal resurrection of Jesus Christ.	Denies it; He will come back in another reincarnation, or He has now no need to come back at all.
Believes in personal resurrection and immortality.	The individual person is forever gone upon the next reincarnation.

(Clifford Wilson and John Weldon, *Occult Shock and Psychic Forces*, San Diego: Master Books, 1980, pp. 86-87).

Telepathy

This is often called mental telepathy because it

refers to understanding or communicating thoughts from one mind to another. Many of the near-death experience accounts say that all the people in the spirit world communicate by telepathy, including Jesus.

Even though God is able to do anything He desires, we find an inconsistency with telepathic messages and the biblical account of Jesus on the Mount of Transfiguration. Luke 9:30-31 records that Moses and Elijah "were talking with Him," and "were speaking of His departure." If people who are in the spirit-world or the hereafter do not need to talk in order to communicate to humans, then why did Moses and Elijah speak to Jesus? God does not always tell us why things are as they are, He just tells us what is. What we are finding here, even though God could have done it another way, is the simple act of the three speaking, hearing and seeing one another. There is no evidence that those already departed, as Moses and Elijah were, use telepathy. There is also no evidence that our risen Lord communicated any differently during his post-resurrection appearances from how He had before.

The experiments on telepathy have failed miserably. Telepathy leans toward the occult by assuming human powers more than what God created for man. He created us with voices to speak and ears to hear.

Third Eye

Why do Hindu religionists place a red dot on their forehead, between the eyebrows? It is actually a sacred symbol to represent the third eye. In yoga it represents the sixth chakra, the chakra of the brow. This supposedly influences the "second sight" or the "sixth sense," that of spiritual enlightenment and psychic ability.

We find no evidence in Scripture for a third eye or for psychic abilities. The teaching upholds a message contrary to the gospel of Jesus Christ. It teaches monism, while the Bible teaches monotheism (Deuteronomy 6:4). It teaches an impersonal god, while the Bible teaches a personal God (Matthew 28:19). It teaches we are divine within, while the Bible teaches we are corrupt within (Romans 3:10). It teaches self-salvation, while the Bible teaches salvation through Jesus (Acts 4:12). It teaches working off bad karma, while the Bible teaches salvation by grace through faith and not of works (Ephesians 2:8-9). It teaches reincarnation, while the Bible teaches one life and then the judgment (Hebrews 9:27). It teaches an eternal absorption in the cosmic oneness and loss of personal identity, while the Bible teaches that the saved will know God intimately, as personal resurrected beings for eternity (1 Corinthians 15).

Visualization and Imagery

The human mind is powerful. It is not so powerful that it can create things and control other people in your environment. Visualization and guided imagery are trades of the New Age for healing, creating wealth, changing circumstances, raising consciousness, and a host of other things.

Harper's Encyclopedia on Mystical and Paranormal Experiences explains the techniques:

> Visualization [is] to deliberately bring into manifestation a desire or need by an exercise of picturing the desire or need in the mind's eye; one sits and images the end-result of the request in mundane form; the picture will eventually become a thought-form strong enough to manifest in the outer world; 1. requires inner mental discipline to not cloud one's mind with how one could or could not attain this desire or need; thought-forms use directions for totality to manifest, and interference from the individual confuses the direction of the atoms; 2. picture should be clear and exact as to the final product and allowed to build up in the etheric world by holding it as

long as possible; repeated sessions are necessary; manifestations will happen more quickly if exercise is performed directly after meditation or in an alpha state of consciousness where the subconscious mind accepts it; 3. can be preformed for one's self or for others; usable for manifesting an increase in prosperity, improvement in health, harmony between two persons, being able to speak in public, etc.; e.g., if one desires a new car, one might visualize a new car parked in the garage and the keys in one's purse or pocket (p. 669).

An obvious danger in this is the occultic overtone of controlling other people against their will in order to meet personal need (or greed). I can control a hammer, but my visualization cannot keep a nail from bending. I can balance my checkbook, but my visualization cannot control the bank to be error-free on my behalf. There are a number of places where imagery and visualization falls short of Scripture. God did not create us as "little creators," this detracts from Him being the sole Creator (Genesis 1:1). God did not give our minds the ability to control others; rather, He calls us to see others as better than ourselves (Philippians 2:1-4). The Bible does not encourage imagery, but tells us to cast down every imagination that opposes God (2 Corinthians 10:5).

7

Occult Groups
and
Spiritism

The occult has been around since the earliest of times. There are some modern groups that are organized as churches whose sole manner of worship and practice centers on the occult.

Association of Research and Enlightenment (A.R.E.)

A man who has caused considerable controversy in the twentieth century with his prophetic utterings is Edgar Cayce, known as the sleeping prophet because of the prophecies he gave while he appeared to be sleeping.

Born in Kentucky in 1877, Cayce realized at an early age that he was clairvoyant, and he was determined to use his gift for the betterment of mankind. At the age of twenty-one Cayce was struck with paralysis of the throat, losing most of his ability to speak. After some time Cayce diagnosed his disease and prescribed a cure while in a self-induced trance. The word quickly spread of the strange ability he possessed.

Cayce began to diagnose illnesses and prescribe cures for people who were thousands of miles away. He would make remarkable diagnoses which were later verified by medical authorities. All this was accomplished in spite of the fact that Cayce had no medical training and only a grammar school education.

Sometimes during his trances he would speak about religious and philosophical issues, and occasionally he would predict the future. During his career his readings on medical questions totalled almost 15,000.

Cayce was active in the Christian church, faithfully reading his Bible from beginning to end each year for forty-six years. However, at the same time, he was an occult practitioner who gained international fame for his exploits.

In 1931 Cayce formed a foundation which he named the Association of Research and Enlightenment, Inc. The purpose of A.R.E. was the preservation and study of the readings of Edgar Cayce. Cayce's son, Hugh Lynn, assumed leadership of the organization upon his father's death in 1945. The A.R.E. did not stagnate after its founder's death, but instead used his readings and experiences as a vast resource for reaching the contemporary world.

Today's aggressively evangelistic A.R.E. claims to offer a contemporary and mature view of the reality of extrasensory perception, the importance of dreams, the logic of reincarnation, a rational or loving personal concept of God, the practical use of prayer and meditation, and a deeper understanding of the Bible (William J. Peterson, *Those Curious New Cults*, New Canaan, CN: Keats Publishing, Inc., 1973, 1975, p. 48). Current paid membership in the A.R.E. totals 20,000, but Cayce's books have sold hundreds of thousands of copies, which brings about a wider following for his work.

Cayce's Readings

The readings made by Cayce over the years reveal not only cures for medical ailments, but also statements about God and the future. His readings brought out the following:

- California would fall into the Pacific Ocean in the early 1970s.
- Jesus Christ was a reincarnation of Adam, Melchizedek, Joshua and other figures who lived before Him.
- God has in His nature a male and female principle, making Him a Father-Mother God.
- Mary, the mother of Jesus, was virgin-born like her Son.
- God does not know the future.
- Salvation is something man does on his own. It is not a work of God alone.
- Reincarnation occurs in many human beings.
- Jesus was tutored in prophecy on Mt. Carmel while He was a teenager. His teacher was a woman named Judy, a leader of the Essenes.
- Jesus grew up in Capernaum, not Nazareth.
- Luke did not write the Acts of the Apostles as traditionally believed by the church. The true author was Cayce himself in a previous life as Lucius, Bishop of Laodicea.

Biblical Evaluation

Although the A.R.E. claims to be a study group and not a religion, the readings made by Cayce comment on God and consequently should be evaluated in the light of God's revealed Word, the Bible.

First and foremost, Edgar Cayce is a false prophet according to biblical standards. He predicted many things which did not come to pass.

> When a prophet speaks in the Name of the LORD, if the thing does not come about or come true, that is the thing which the Lord has not spoken. The prophet has spoken it presumptuously; you shall not be afraid of him (Deuteronomy 18:22).

When Cayce said God does not know the future, he clearly contradicted Scripture. In stark contrast to Cayce, the God of the Bible does know the future, telling mankind of events before they come to pass.

> I declared the former things long ago and they went forth from My mouth, and I proclaimed them. Suddenly I acted, and they came to pass . . . Therefore I declared them to you long ago, before they took place I proclaimed them to you, lest you should say, "My idol has done them, and my graven image and my molten image have commanded them" (Isaiah 48:3,5).

The God of the Bible revealed through His prophets many things in detail before they came to pass. The predictions were specific and always accurate. Contrast that to Cayce, whose predictions were vague and often inaccurate.

There is no evidence that Jesus studied prophecy on Mt. Carmel or was a member of the Essenes. The teachings of Jesus came not from men but from God the Father:

> Jesus therefore said, "When you lift up the Son of Man, then you will know that I am He, and I do nothing on My own initiative, but I speak these things as the Father taught Me" (John 8:28).

Cayce and his followers have a low view of the Person and work of Jesus Christ. One Cayce devotee expressed it this way:

> For almost twenty centuries the moral sense of the Western World has been blunted by a theology which teaches the vicarious atonement of sin through Christ, the Son of God . . . All men and women are sons of God . . . Christ's giving of his life . . . is no unique event in history . . . To build these two statements, therefore—that Christ was the Son of God and that he died for man's salvation—into a dogma, and then to make salvation depend upon believing in that dogma, has been the great psychological crime because it places responsibility for redemption on something external to the self; it makes salvation dependent on belief in the divinity of another person rather than on self-transformation through belief in one's own intrinsic divinity (quoted in Phillip Swihart, *Reincarnation, Edgar Cayce and the Bible,* Downers Grove, IL: InterVarsity Press, 1975, pp. 27-28).

Cayce's claim to be the reincarnated author of the book of Acts rests on his fundamental belief in reincarnation. This is one of the central doctrines and greatest attractions of the A.R.E. If one disproves reincarnation, the validity of the A.R.E. is forever destroyed.

Edgar Cayce cannot be considered a prophet of God. Although he faithfully read his Bible and was active in church, his readings contradicted every sacred belief of Christianity. The A.R.E. which Cayce founded has continued in his anti-Christian beliefs and should also be avoided.

Mediums and Seances

Mediums usually claim to have a spirit-guide who is their initial and primary contact in the spirit world. The spirit-guide supposedly puts the medium in contact with the spirits of the departed ones. The sessions conducted by the medium are known as seances.

In the book *The Challenging Counterfeit*, the author Raphael Gasson, a former medium, warns of the subtle yet deep dangers of spiritualism. Gasson discusses the apparitions he called up which he believes were not spirits of the dead but demonic deception. While a spiritualist medium, Gasson believed the following:

> As a former spiritualist minister and active medium, it is possible for them to say that at the time of my participation in the movement, I actually believed that these spirits were the spirits of the departed dead and that it was my duty to preach this to all those with whom I came into contact day by day (*The Challenging Counterfeit*, Plainfield, NJ: Logos Books, 1970, p. 36).

On the abilities of a medium:

> It is possible for the medium to give a demonstration of his gift at any seance or public meeting, in a bus, train, restaurant or park. It does not require any special lighting and can be demonstrated anywhere. No form of trance condition is necessary, only the tuning in to the spirit world by the medium, who being in a passive state of mind is open to receive messages from those who presume to be the spirits of the dead (ibid., p. 36).

Other prominent spiritists have included Sir Arthur Conan Doyle (creator of Sherlock Holmes); philosopher and psychic, William James; and the "father" of British Spiritism, Sir Oliver Lodge.

Bishop Pike

Spiritism came to the forefront in the 1960s when Episcopal Bishop James Pike attempted to contact the spirit of his dead son. Pike's son had committed suicide, and the Bishop consulted several mediums in an attempt to contact him.

While on television in Toronto, Canada, Pike met with famous medium Arthur Ford, who through his spirit-guide gave the Bishop the following message from his son: "He wants you to definitely understand that neither you nor any other member of the family has any right to feel any sense of guilt or have any feelings that you failed him in any way" (James A. Pike with Diane Kennedy, *The Other Side: An Account of My Experiences With Psychic Phenomena*, New York: Doubleday, 1968, pp. 246-247).

Pike, according to his own words, had "jettisoned the Trinity, the Virgin Birth and the Incarnation," and had become a believer in the world of departed spirits without any objective criteria by which to test the spirits. The Bishop died two years later after disappearing in the Judean Desert. The mediums in whom Pike had come to trust were giving his wife false comfort between the time he was lost and found dead, saying he was alive but sick in a cave. The Bishop's case became famous and led many into dabbling with spiritism.

The Seance

What happens at the seance? What is it that makes people believe that they are contacting the spirit world? William J. Petersen comments:

Spiritualists say there are six types of seances: passivity, vocal reality, trumpet revelation, lights, transfiguration, and levitation. In one sitting, several of these might be witnessed. One former medium, Victor Ernest, describes it like this: "Seances are noted for quietness. As the participants enter and meditate, they block out their tensions, worries, anxieties and problems... Lights are turned down at every seance. Shades are drawn in the daytime and at night."

Seances always begin on time. If you come late, the spirits might be offended.

After a time of meditation, an object may move. Sometimes it is a glass on the table. Sometimes it is a small board on which a message is automatically written. Then the medium may go into a trance. His body may seem to be possessed by the spirit. When he opens his mouth, the voice you hear is different from the medium's voice. In fact, the entire personality of the medium seems to have changed (*Those Curious New Cults*, New Canaan, CN: Keats Publishing Co., 1973, 1975, p. 63).

During the seance a variety of different phenomena usually occurs, including materialization, speaking through a trumpet, spirit writing, apports and the appearance of ectoplasm.

Materialization

Materialization is the term used for the appearance during the seance of the spirits of the departed in some material form. The obvious question arises, "Are these materializations real?"

Walter B. Gibson observes that materializations are infrequently used today by mediums:

The most spectacular spirit seances are those in which materializations are produced; for if it were genuine, a materialization would be the most convincing form of psychic phenomena possible. Seances of this type have a long tradition, dating back many years. But from the standpoint of the fraudulent medium, while a materialization may be desirable, it is extremely dangerous. Many mediums who have defied detection and trick methods have come to grief when they entered the field of materialization. Supposed spirits have been seized during many a seance and turned out to be living human beings. Police have raided the lairs of false mediums and brought back trick apparatus used in the seances. Most fake mediums now eliminate physical phenomena altogether, and materialization in particular

(*Secrets of Magic*, New York: Grosset and Dunlap, 1967, p. 140).

Trumpet Speaking

A favorite device used in seances is the trumpet through which the spirit supposedly speaks. Although it sounds impressive, it is actually a clever trick. M. Lamar Keene, a former medium who exposed many of the secrets of his trade, reveals how he performed the trumpet phenomenon:

My real contribution to the science and art of mediumship was in creating an original trumpet phenomenon. The standard trumpet sitting takes place in the familiar darkness—sometimes with the red light, sometimes without—and voices heard speaking through the tin megaphone are said to be those of the spirits.

Some mediums just sit or stand in the darkness and talk through the trumpet, but these show little initiative or imagination. Our trumpets had a luminous band so that the sitters could see them whirling around the room, hovering in space, or sometimes swinging back and forth in rhythm with a hymn.

The trick was the old black art business. My partner and I, and other confederates if we needed them, wore head-to-toe black outfits which rendered us invisible in the darkness. We could handle the trumpet with impunity even in a good red light and with the luminescent bands giving off a considerable glow.

Some skeptics, of course, suspected wires or threads, but my special trumpet effect really bamboozled them. It bamboozled everybody and may be justly described as one of the few truly original phenomena in mediumship.

The sitter's experience was of holding the trumpet in his or her hands and feeling it vibrate with the voice sounds. Yet there were no wires, no cords—nothing (*The Psychic Mafia*, New York: St. Martin's Press, 1976, pp. 104-105).

Spirit Writing

A popular manifestation during many seances is the appearance of writing on blank cards, a practice known as spirit writing. The writings are supposedly messages from departed spirits. Spirit writing is another trick of the mediums. M. Lamar Keene reveals:

Among my followers a favorite phenomenon was spirit card writing. Blank cards were given to each sitter, and he or she was asked to sign his or her name. The cards were then collected and placed on a table in the center of the room, and the lights were lowered. A hymn was sung, the lights were turned on, and *voila!* the cards now bore spirit messages, signatures of dead loved ones, Bible verses, poems, personal reminiscences, and other heartwarming evidences of life after death.

There were two ways of doing this. The cards signed by the sitters could be removed from the room in the dark by confederates and the messages added, then returned before the lights were turned on. The other way was to have cards prepared in advance, including look-alike forgeries of the sitters' signatures, and simply switch these for blank cards (ibid., p. 109-110).

Apports

An apport is the sudden appearance of a solid object in or through another solid object. M. Lamar Keene, explains apports:

I was also a whiz at apports. These were gifts from the spirits: sometimes they were worthless trinkets like rings or brooches; other times, more impressively, they were (as I've already described) objects we had stolen from the sitter.

The apports, as previously described, sometimes arrived in full light and other times tumbled out of the trumpet in the dark. In exotic variations I arranged for apports to turn up in a newly baked cake, in a sandwich, or inside a shoe.

Table Tilting

Harry Houdini, the great escape artist, who was also a psychic investigator, had this to say concerning table tilting:

> The echoes by which fake mediums do their tricks would fill a volume . . . Of course, so long as edicts insist on working in darkness or semi-obscurity, adequate investigations will be almost impossible. In the dimness, it is easy for the spirit-invoked to lift a table by means of a piece of steel projecting from his sleeve, or with a steel hook hidden in his vest (Houdini and Dunninger, *Magic and Mystery*, op. cit. pp. 30-31).

Spirit Raps

It has already been mentioned that modern spiritism got its start when the Fox sisters created spirit rapping by secretly snapping their toe joints. Consequently, other mediums have felt it necessary to produce the same manifestation. There have been a variety of different methods employed to produce this desired effect, with the raps usually coming from the table where the medium is seated.

Walter B. Gibson reveals some of the ways these mysterious raps are produced:

> With some tables, raps may be made by rubbing the side of a shoe against the table leg, the sound carrying up into the top of the table. There are old, creaky tables that are especially suited to imitation spirit raps because of their loose joints. The medium can produce raps in a slightly darkened room by careful pressure on the table top, causing noise like snaps to come from the table.
>
> Noticeable raps may be produced by setting the finger tips firmly against the top of a table. The left thumb presses against the table, and the right thumbnail is pushed against the left thumbnail. This produces an audible click, and there are fraudulent mediums who

have caused a succession of mysterious raps in this simple manner, without detection.

Mechanical table rappers make the best sounds ... The top of a center-legged table is hollowed out to receive an electric coil. Two wires run through the table leg and terminate in projecting points which come out of the bottom of one of the small legs. Concealed beneath the carpet, at different places in the room, are metal floor plates. Wires run from these to an adjoining room, where they are controlled by a push button (*Secrets*, op. cit., pp. 133-134).

Spirit Photography

Most forms of psychic phenomena, although spectacular in nature, leave no lasting evidence. This is not true, however, in the case of spirit photography which supposedly offers material proof that the spirits of the dead appeared in the seance.

A spirit photograph is an ordinary photograph taken during the seance, and when developed, it reveals the faces of the dead surrounding the sitter. This photograph is offered as proof the spirits were present. However, this is another clever mediumistic trick. Walter B. Gibson reveals how this deception is accomplished:

Back in the days of the Civil War, a photographer discovered that if an old plate was improperly cleaned, and used again, a faint trace of the original picture would remain. That was the method used in the early stages of the game, but in later years spirit photographers have allowed their subjects to bring their own plates and to watch them being developed. Still spirit forms appear, and people pay large sums for such photographs (ibid., p. 146).

Ectoplasm

The *Dictionary of Mysticism* defines ectoplasm:

Ectoplasm: A term coined by Professor Richet (a contraction of the Greek words *ektos*, exteriorized, and *plasma*, substance) for the mysterious protoplasmic substance which streams forth from the bodies of mediums, producing super-physical phenomena, including materializations, under manipulation by a discarnate intelligence. Ectoplasm is described as a matter which is invisible and impalpable in its primary state, but assuming the state of a vapor, liquid or solid, according to its stage of condensation. It emits an ozone-like smell. The ectoplasm is considered by spiritualists to be the materialization of the astral body (p. 53).

However, the production of ectoplasm can be easily manufactured by the medium. The ex-medium, M. Lamar Keene, explains how he created the ectoplasm effect:

It's amazing what effects can be created in the dark, manipulating yards and yards of chiffon and gauze which appear to shimmer in the unearthly glow of the ruby light. What I did was what magicians call "black art." The parts of me not covered by ectoplasm were garbed totally in black and were quite invisible in the dark.

Standing in the seance room in my invisible outfit, I would deftly unroll a ball of chiffon out to the middle of the floor and manipulate it until eventually it enveloped me. What the sitters saw was a phenomenon: A tiny ball of ectoplasm sending out shimmering tendrils which gradually grew or developed into a fully materialized spirit. Unless you have witnessed the effect under seance conditions, you'll find it hard to grasp how eerily convincing it can be.

The ectoplasmic figure could disappear the same way it appeared. I simply unwound the chiffon from my body slowly and dramatically then wadded it back into the original tiny ball. What the sitter saw was the fully formed spirit gradually disintegrate, evaporate into a puff of ectoplasm.

The variations were endless (Keene, *Psychic Mafia,* op. cit., p. 101).

Proskauer in his chapter, "Ectoplasm is Bunk," gives some excellent illustrations and examples of the fraud involved in ectoplasm (ibid., pp. 90-98).

Is It All Deception?

Harry Houdini and Joseph Dunninger exposed in their day the fraudulent practices of mediums. More recently Keene revealed his deception of untold thousands. These individuals, along with others who are well qualified in spiritistic phenomena, believe all such practice is deception. They strongly assert that spirits of the dead do not talk to the one sitting at the seance but rather that the medium is perpetrating a con game.

We also believe the great majority of things which happen during a seance can be rationally explained as deception. However, we likewise believe that supernatural manifestation sometimes occurs.

John Warwick Montgomery makes an appropriate comment:

Almost everyone has heard of the clever techniques of fraudulent mediums—such as inflatable rubber gloves that leave the impressions of the spirit hands in paraffin and then, deflated, are able to be drawn out of the hardened wax through a small hole, leaving nothing but ghostly imprints. Houdini claimed that he could duplicate by natural means any spiritistic phenomenon shown to him. And recent visitors to Disneyland have invariably been impressed by the computerized effectiveness of the "spirits" in the Haunted Mansion. Are not all occult phenomena capable of similar explanation?

Doubtless the world would be a more comfortable and secure place if the answer were yes; unfortunately, however, such an answer is not possible. Innumerable instances of occult phenomena resist categorization as "humbug" or natural occurrences in disguise (John Warwick Montgomery, *Principalities and Powers*, Minneapolis, MN: Bethany Fellowship, Inc., 1973, p. 30).

Can the Dead Communicate With the Living?

If there is any supernatural activity in the seance, it is most certainly *not* in the spirit of the departed one speaking through the medium. It is not possible, according to the Scriptures, to contact the spirits of the dead. Jesus made this very clear with the account of the rich man and Lazarus.

Now there was a certain rich man, and he habitually dressed in purple and fine linen, gaily living in splendor every day. And a certain poor man named Lazarus was laid at his gate, covered with sores, and longing to be fed with the crumbs which were falling from the rich man's table; besides, even the dogs were coming and licking his sores. Now it came about that the poor man died and he was carried away by the angels to Abraham's bosom; and the rich man also died and was buried. And in Hades he lifted up his eyes, being in torment, and saw Abraham far away, and Lazarus in his bosom. And he cried out and said, "Father Abraham, have mercy on me, and send Lazarus, that he may dip the tip of his finger in water and cool off my tongue; for I am in agony in this flame." But Abraham said, "Child, remember that during your life you received your good things, and likewise Lazarus bad things; but now he is being comforted here, and you are in agony. And besides all this, between us and you there is a great chasm fixed, in order that those who wish to come over from here to you may not be able, and that none may cross over from there to us." And he said, "Then I beg you, Father, that you send him to my father's house—for I have five brothers—that he may warn them, lest they also come to this place of torment." But Abraham said, "They have Moses and the Prophets; let them hear them." But he said, "No, Father Abraham, but if someone goes to them from the dead,

they will repent!" But he said to him, "If they do not listen to Moses and the Prophets, neither will they be
persuaded if someone rises from the dead" (Luke 16:19-
31).

Two things need to be noted about this passage:

1. There is a great gulf fixed between the abode of
   the righteous dead and the unrighteous dead
   which no one can cross. The dead, in other words,
   are limited in their movement.

2. The rich man was refused permission to warn his
   five brothers of their impending fate if they did
   not repent. The passage indicates, along with the
   rest of Scripture, that the dead are not allowed to
   speak to the living on any matter. The response in
   this case was that the brothers needed to believe
   what God had said to escape their doom rather
   than a voice from the dead.

Jesus declared that those who harden their hearts
against the very words of God through Moses and the
Prophets would not listen to one returned from the
dead. This is proven by those who reject the gospel of
Jesus Christ today. Jesus Christ *did* rise from the dead,
and yet people still reject His Word.

Medium at Endor

A passage of Scripture often quoted in discussions
of mediums is 1 Samuel 28, the story of Saul and the
medium at Endor. Proponents of spiritism cite the passage to point out that the medium was able to contact
Samuel's spirit.

First, it must be stated that not all Bible scholars
believe it was Samuel who was called up; some believe
it was a demon, and some believe that it was a trick. But
the majority of evangelical scholars hold that it actually

was Samuel (Joseph Bayly, *What About Horoscopes?*, Elgin, IL: David C. Cook Publishing Company, 1970, p. 71). This position can be substantiated and explained by studying the context.

First, the element of surprise by the medium indicates she was just as surprised as anyone at Samuel's appearance (verse 12).

Second, the Scripture clearly indicates that Samuel appeared (verse 12). There is no indication that either fraud or demonism is present, as should be the case if those were true.

Thus, the logical conclusion must be in keeping with Scripture. The Bible teaches that men have no power to call up dead spirits, yet Samuel did appear. One concludes that it was God who chose to raise up Samuel for this one occasion for His purposes, and there was no doubt who it was. Neither the powers of darkness (the medium) nor the poor representation of the Kingdom of Light (Saul) had any doubt as to the identity of who appeared.

God always does as He chooses in this area, just as He chose to bring back Moses and Elijah on the Mount of Transfiguration before Christ was resurrected. By means of analogy, it is also true that though all men are subject to death, neither Enoch nor Elijah died. There again, the Lord made the exception.

The Scripture speaks loud and clear in its denunciation of any type of spiritistic practice.

You shall not allow a sorceress to live (Exodus 22:18).

You shall not eat anything with the blood nor practice divination or soothsaying (Leviticus 19:26).

Do not turn to mediums or spiritists; do not seek them out to be defiled by them. I am the LORD Your God (Leviticus 19:31).

As for the person who turns to mediums and to

spiritists, to play the harlot after them, I will also set My face against that person and will cut him off from among his people (Leviticus 20:6).

Now a man or a woman who is a medium or spiritist shall surely be put to death. They shall be stoned with stones, their bloodguiltiness is upon them (Leviticus 20:27).

When you enter the land which the LORD your God gives you, you shall not learn to imitate the detestable things of those nations. There shall not be found among you anyone who makes his son or his daughter pass through the fire, one who uses divination, one who practices witchcraft, or one who interprets omens, or a sorcerer, or one who casts a spell, or a medium or a spiritist, or one who calls up the dead. For whoever does these things is destable to the LORD; and because of these detestable things the LORD your God will drive them out before you (Deuteronomy 18:9-12).

And when they say to you, "Consult the mediums and the spiritists who whisper and mutter," should not a people consult their God? Should they consult the dead on behalf of the living? (Isaiah 8:19).

Rosicrucianism

The true origin of Rosicrucianism is unknown. Today there are two groups which claim to be representative of Rosicrucianism and each claims a different origin. The Rosicrucian Fellowship is headquartered in Oceanside, California, and attempts to trace its origin back to the Chaldeans: "The founders of the Rosicrucian system were originally identical with the Chaldeans" (R. Swinburne Clymer, *The Secret Schools*, Oceanside, CA: Philos Publishing, p. 16).

The rival organization, the Ancient Mystical Order Rosae Crucis (abbreviated AMORC), headquartered in San Jose, California, dubiously "traces its origin to the mystery schools or secret schools of learning established during the reign of Thutmose III, about 1500 B.C. in Egypt" (*Who and What Are the Rosicrucians?*, p. 8).

This latter group is adamant about being the faithful Rosicrucian order. One of their pamphlets states: "There is but one international Rosicrucian order operating throughout the world . . . This organization does not sponsor a few modern publishing houses, or book propositions, operating under similar names, or selling instructions or books under the name of Rosicrucian fellowship, society, fraternity and other similar titles" (Anon., *Why Are We Here? and Why Are Our Lives Unequal?*, San Jose, California; The Rosicrucian Press, Ltd., 1952, p. 10).

The earliest authentically Rosicrucian writings come from the seventeenth century. These are anonymous works entitled *Fama Fraternitatis* and *The Confessions of the Order*. These works set forth the travels of the alleged founder of the order, one Christian Rosenkreutz.

As the story goes, Rosenkreutz (1378-1484) learned secrets about medicine and magic while on a pilgrimage to the Near East. On his return to Europe, he attempted to share his new knowledge with the world, but his teachings were rejected by the unenlightened public. He then founded a secret fraternity whose members communicated by secret-coded writings.

Upon his death, Rosenkreutz was buried in the house in which the Order met. More than 100 years after his death his grave was opened and, along with his supposed unconsumed body, occultic writings were found. The Order was founded in 1614, based on the supposed true wisdom and knowledge discovered by Rosenkreutz.

Most scholars agree the story is mythical, but it gives the Order the appearance of historical source. In fact, the author of the Rosenkreutz story later identified himself as Valentine Andrea and then finally admitted that the whole story was fictitious. However, this was not the end of the secret movement:

> Even this disclosure, however, did not prevent many enthusiastic persons from continuing to believe in the reality of Rosicrucian brotherhood, and professing to be acquainted with its secrets (Rev. James Gardner, *The Faiths of the World*, Volume 2, London: A Fullarton and Co., 1874, p. 775).

What is Rosicrucianism?

The following excerpts from a Rosicrucian writing explains the Rosicrucians' purpose:

> In general terms we may announce that the primary object of Rosicrucianism is to elucidate the mysteries that encompass us in life, and reverently to raise the veil from those that await us in the dreaded dominions of death (R. Swinburne Clymer, op. cit., p. 8).

The Rosicrucian Order is syncretistic, meaning that it borrows ideas and beliefs from divergent and sometimes opposing sources, attempting to unify those ideas and beliefs into a coherent world view. Rosicrucians, for all their divergent beliefs, all unify under the central tenet that esoteric wisdom about life beyond the grave has been preserved through the ages and is revealed only to those within the secret brotherhood. Charles Braden observed:

> There are Rosicrucian societies, fraternities, orders, fellowships or lodges in most countries of the modern world. Some of them are very active; others are obscure and highly secret; some seem primarily religious in their emphasis, and some categorically deny that Rosicrucianism is a religion, holding rather that it is a philosophy, making use of the most modern scientific

methods and techniques, as well as the methods of the occultist, the mystic and the seer, in the quest for truth.

But, while Rosicrucianism is sectarian in character and the various branches are sometimes bitterly critical of each other, they do have common features, the central one being the purported possession of certain secret wisdom handed down from ancient times, through a secret brotherhood, an esoteric wisdom that can only be imparted to the initiated (Charles Braden, "Rosicrucianism," *Encyclopedia Britannica*, 1964 ed., XIX, p. 558).

The Teachings of Rosicrucianism

Although one of the attractions of Rosicrucianism is its claim that it is not a religion, its writings contain specific religious teaching which denies every cardinal doctrine of Christianity.

The Bible

The Rosicrucian Order does not hold the Bible in any special favor. R. Swinburne Clymer writes, "All secret and sacred writings have truth in them, irrespective of their source, and must be judged by their inculcations rather than the source" (R. Swinburne Clymer, op. cit., p. 19).

Jesus Christ

- "Jesus was born of *Gentile* parents through whose veins flowed Aryan blood" (p. 53).

- Jesus did not die on the cross, for "an examination of the body revealed that Jesus was *not dead*. The blood *flowing from the wounds* proved that His body was not lifeless" (p. 265).

- The Ascension is rejected because "there is nothing in the original accounts of it to warrant the belief that Jesus arose physically or in His physical body in a cloud into the heavens" (p. 283).

- And finally, it is claimed that Rosicrucian archival records "clearly show that after Jesus retired to the monastery at Carmel He lived for many years, and carried on secret missions with His apostles" (p. 289). (H. Spencer Lewis, *The Mystical Life of Jesus*, Eighth edition, 1948).

None of the above claims by the Rosicrucians concerning Jesus Christ conforms to the Bible. Matthew 1:1-18 and Luke 3:23-38 affirm the long Jewish ancestry of the human nature of Jesus Christ. Acts 2:23,24 clearly shows that the death of Jesus Christ on the cross was according to the predetermined plan of God.

St. Paul reminds us that "if Christ has not been raised, your faith is worthless; you are still in your sins" (1 Corinthians 15:17). Finally, Acts 1:9-11 and Matthew 24:30 confirm Christ's ascension into heaven and His eventual public (not secret) return to earth. The Jesus Christ of the Rosicrucians is not the Jesus Christ of the Bible.

Salvation

Rosicrucianism does not teach that a person should trust Christ and Him *alone* for his eternal salvation. Their system is one of self-effort, their motto being, "TRY." They believe Jesus Christ never died for the sins of the world but that such teachings were added to the Bible by the Church at the Council of Nicea in 326 A.D. (see R. Swinburne Clymer op. cit., p. 18). Clymer also states: "Man through his own individual and consciously-made efforts must attain spiritual enlightenment and ultimate immortality" (ibid., p. 19).

The Bible doctrine of salvation states that salvation is only, and completely, by grace. In fact, Paul states:

> Now to the one who works, his wage is not reckoned as a favor, but as what is due. But to the one who does not work, but believes in Him who justifies the ungodly, his faith is reckoned as righteousness, just as David also speaks of the blessing upon the man to whom God reckons righteousness apart from works (Romans 4:4-6).

Occultic Influence

Kurt Koch cites a German Rosicrucian pamphlet, *Meisterung des Lebens*, which reveals its occultic teachings.

> Things are made even clearer elsewhere in the booklet. The page is entitled: "The Secret World Within Us. Abilities Which We Know of and Ought to Use."
>
> What abilities are these?
>
> (1) "By touching letters and other objects we can become the recipients of painful messages." This is psychometry, a form of extra-sensory perception.
>
> (2) "Thoughts or sense-impressions can be transmitted at a distance." This is an occult form of mental suggestion.
>
> (3) "Our consciousness can suddenly see far-off places and events." This is clairvoyance by means of psychic powers.
>
> (4) "Some people reveal their true character by magnetic radiation." This is the spiritists' idea of the so-called "aura."
>
> In this booklet *Meisterung des Lebens*, therefore, the Order of Rosicrucians encourages its members to take up psychic and occultic practices (Kurt Koch, *Occult ABC*, Grand Rapids, MI: Kregel Publications, n.d., p. 193).

Rosicrucianism does not call itself a religion but rather a secret society which "expounds a system of metaphysical and physical philosophy intended to awaken the dormant, latent faculties of the individual whereby he may utilize to a better advantage his natural talents and lead a happier and more useful life" (*Who and What Are the Rosicrucians?*, p. 3).

However, Rosicrucianism does speak about religious matters and denies every central doctrine of the Christian faith. There are strong occultic teachings in Rosicrucianism, something the Bible soundly condemns. Like Freemasonry, Rosicrucianism holds many of its practices in secret, which is in contrast to Christianity and the open and public nature of its proclamation.

One who desires to serve Jesus Christ and His Kingdom has no business belonging to the Rosicrucian Order, working in darkness. Rather he should shout the message of Jesus Christ from the roof tops, as the Bible exhorts us: "What I tell you in the darkness, speak in the light; and what you hear whispered in your ear, proclaim upon the housetops" (Matthew 10:27).

Spiritism (Necromancy)

Spiritism (sometimes called spiritualism) is the oldest form of religious counterfeit known to man. Its roots go back to the beginning of time. The Bible speaks of spiritistic practices occuring in ancient Egypt. The Book of Exodus records the Egyptians' many occultic activities, including magic, sorcery and speaking to the dead (Exodus 7 and 8).

What is spiritism? A secular book, *The Dictionary of Mysticism*, defines spiritualism (spiritism) as:

The science, philosophy and religion of continuous life, based upon the demonstrated fact of communication, by means of mediumship, with those who live in the spirit world. Spiritualism rejects the belief in the physical reincarnation, but teaches that death is a new birth into a spiritual body, without any change in individuality and character, and without impairment of memory (Frank Gaynor, ed., *Dictionary of Mysticism*, New York: Citadel Press, n.d., p. 174).

The main idea behind spiritism is that the spirits of the dead have the capacity to communicate with people here on earth through mediums, individuals who act as intermediaries between the material world and the spirit world. We do not use the term spiritualism because we do not believe such practices are actually "spiritual" or approved by God. We prefer the term "spiritism," since we believe authentic mediums contact evil spirits only posing as the spirits of the dead.

Spiritism has continued on through the ages, though sometimes waning in popularity. More than 100 years ago it experienced a rebirth which has grown and now blossomed into the modern-day spiritistic movement.

The Fox Sisters

Spiritism, in its modern form, had its beginning in the United States in 1847 through two American women, Margaret and Kate Fox. When John D. Fox and his family moved into a house in Hydeville, New York, the two youngest children, Margaret and Kate, began to hear knockings in various parts of the house.

At first it was thought this was coming from mice, but when other strange phenomena were reported, like furniture moving around by itself, natural explanations seemed inadequate. Young Kate tried to contact the "spirit" which was causing all the commotion. When she snapped her fingers, there was a mysterious knock in response.

Kate and Margaret devised a way to communicate with the alleged spirit which replied to their questions by coded rappings. The spirit said he was Charles Rosma, who supposedly had been murdered by a former tenant of the Fox home. When portions of the human skeleton were actually found in the cellar, worldwide attention was given to the Fox sisters.

Many groups, including scientists, who investigated the Fox sisters and the rappings went away baffled. Among those who investigated was the famous New York editor Horace Greeley ("Go West, Young Man, Go West"). Greeley concluded that "whatever may be the origin or cause of the rappings, the ladies in whose presence they occur do not make them."

In 1886 the Fox sisters confessed that they were frauds. The raps were produced by cracking their toe joints. Margaret conducted a series of demonstrations showing how she did it. At the New York Academy of Music, Margaret Fox stood on a small pine table on the stage in her stocking feet and produced loud distinct raps that could be heard throughout the building.

The Beliefs of Spiritism

Some of the official writings of spiritism claim compatibility with Christianity.

How—it may be asked—should Christianity be opposed to spiritualism when the Christian religion was really born in a seance? The real beginning of Christianity, its motive power, its great impetus, came—not from the birth or death of Jesus—but from Pentecost, the greatest seance in history (R.F. Austin, *The A.B.C. of Spiritualism*, Milwaukee, WI: National Spiritualist Association of Churches, n.d., p. 23).

However, a comparison between the beliefs of spiritism and Christianity show no agreement whatsoever. The following questions and answers are taken from a booklet distributed by the National Spiritualist Association of Churches:

Is not spiritualism based upon the Bible? (Q. 11)

No. The Bible so far as it is inspired and true, is based upon mediumship and therefore, both Christianity ... and spiritualism rest on the same basis.

Spiritualism does not depend for its credentials and proofs upon any former revelation.

Do spiritualists believe in the divinity of Jesus? (Q. 16)

Most assuredly. They believe in the divinity of all men. Every man is divine in that he is a child of God, and inherits a spiritual (divine) nature ...

Does spiritualism recognize Jesus as one person of the Trinity, co-equal with the Father, and divine in a sense in which divinity is unattainable by other men? (Q. 17)

No. Spiritualism accepts him as one of many Saviour Christs, who at different times have come into the world to lighten its darkness and show by precept and example the way of life to men. It recognizes him as a world Saviour but not as "the only name" given under heaven by which men can be saved.

Does not spiritualism recognize special value and efficacy in the death of Jesus in saving men (Q. 19)?

No. Spiritualism sees in the death of Jesus an illustration of the martyr spirit, of that unselfish and heroic devotion to humanity which ever characterized the life of Jesus, but no special atoning value in his sufferings and death ...

From the standpoint of spiritualism, how is the character and work of Jesus to be interpreted? (Q.21)

Jesus was a great Mediator, or Medium who recognized all the fundamental principles of spiritualism and practiced them ...

Does spiritualism recognize rewards and punishments in the life after death? (Q. 86)

No man escapes punishment, no man misses due reward. The idea of atoning sacrifice for sins which will remove their natural consequences (pardon) is simply ludicrous to the inhabitants of the spirit spheres.

Do the departed, according to spiritualism, find heaven and hell as depicted by Church teachings? (Q. 88)

Not at all . . . They deny any vision of a great white throne, any manifestations of a personal God, any appearance of Jesus, or any lake of fire and torment for lost souls (cited by Edmond Gruss, *Cults and the Occult*, rev. ed., Grand Rapids, MI: Baker Book House, 1974, pp. 57-58).

The Bible and Spiritism

Attempting to contact the spirits of the dead is not only fruitless, it also leads one down the path of death. M. Lamar Keene reveals the reason he quit his profession:

If I stayed in mediumship I saw only deepening gloom. All the mediums I've known or known about have had tragic endings.

The Fox sisters, who started it all, wound up as alcoholic derelicts. William Slade, famed for his slate-writing tricks, died insane in a Michigan sanitarium. Margery, the medium, lay on her deathbed a hopeless drunk. The celebrated Arthur Ford fought the battle of the bottle to the very end and lost. And the inimitable Mable Riffle, boss of Camp Chesterfield—well, when she died it was winter and freezing cold, and her body had to be held until a thaw for burial; the service was in the cathedral of Chesterfield. Very few attended.

Wherever I looked it was the same: mediums at the end of a tawdry life (ibid., pp. 147-148).

What a contrast this is to the life that is offered by Jesus Christ. Jesus promised, "I came that they might have life, and might have it abundantly" (John 10:10). The Christian, rather than attempting the hopeless task of talking to the dead, can talk to the living God. He does not need to resort to mediums or spiritists.

Moreover, those who have died having a relationship with God are not dead but are spiritually alive in God's presence. Jesus pointed this out:

> But regarding the resurrection of the dead, have you not read that which was spoken to God saying, I am the God of Abraham, and the God of Isaac, and the God of Jacob? He is not the God of the dead but of the living (Matthew 22:31,32).

Jesus Christ offers real hope. Spiritists offer false hope that leads to the path of destruction. Contrast the bitter end of mediums and spiritists with that of a man of God, the apostle Paul, who gave this dying declaration:

> I have fought the good fight, I have finished the course, I have kept the faith; in the future there is laid up for me the crown of righteousness, which the Lord the righteous Judge, will award to me on that day; and not only to me, but also to all who have loved his appearing (2 Timothy 4:7,8).

8

Satan
and
Demons

Satan

Satan, or the devil, has been the subject of a multitude of books and discussions for thousands of years. Some deny his existence, saying that he is merely a mythological figure. Others seem obsessed with him, seeing him behind everything imaginable.

We will explore answers to these questions: Is there such a creature? If so, what powers does he have? Who is he? Where did he come from? Should Christians fear him?

He Does Exist

The devil is real. He is not a figment of one's imagination or a mere symbol of evil; he has personal existence! He had a beginning; he is at work now. But eventually he will be judged by God. How do we know he exists?

Since it is our firm conviction that the Bible is a supernatural revelation from the true and living God, correct in everything it affirms, we can go to the Bible and see what it says about the devil and his plans.

The evangelist Billy Sunday was once asked, "Why do you believe the devil exists?"

He replied, "There are two reasons: one, because the Bible says so; two, because I've done business with him."

The Career of Satan

The career of Satan begins in the distant past. God created a multitude of angels to do His bidding. In the angelic rank there was one angel who was given the highest position, guardian to the Throne of the Most High. His name was Lucifer.

Lucifer

Information about Lucifer is revealed to us in Ezekiel 28:11-19. This passage is addressed to the prince of Tyre, a man who was vain because of the wealth he possessed and thought himself to be God. While God is rebuking the prince of Tyre for his vanity, He also introduces another character called the king of Tyre, the real motivator of the prince of Tyre.

> Again the word of the LORD came to me saying, "Son of man, take up a lamentation over the king of Tyre and say to him, 'Thus says the Lord GOD, "you had the seal of perfection, full of wisdom and perfect in beauty. You were in Eden, the garden of God; every precious stone was your covering: the ruby, the topaz, and the diamond; the beryl, the onyx, and the jasper; the lapis lazuli, the turquoise, and the emerald; and the gold, the workmanship of your settings and sockets, was in you. On the day

you were created they were prepared. You were the anointed cherub who covers, and I placed you there. You were on the holy mountain of God; you walked in the midst of the stones of fire. You were blameless in your ways from the day you were created, until unrighteousness was found in you" ' " (Ezekiel 28:11-15).

In his doctrinal treatise, *Satan*, Lewis Sperry Chafer comments:

According to the Scriptures, the supreme motive of Satan is his purpose to become like the Most High and, though that purpose was formed even before the age of man, it has been his constant actuating motive from that time until now. It is also the teaching of the Scriptures that Satan is in especial authority in the present age; he being permitted the exercise of his own power in order that he, and all his followers, may make their final demonstration to the whole universe of the utter folly of their claims and of their abject helplessness when wholly independent of their Creator. This is definitely predicted in 2 Timothy 3:9 as the final outcome of the attitude of the world in its independence toward God: "They shall proceed no further: for their folly shall be manifest unto all men" (Lewis Sperry Chafer, *Satan*, Philadelphia, PA: Sunday School Times Co., 1972, p. 73).

The king of Tyre is Lucifer. He was perfect in all his ways, the highest ranking celestial being, the most beautiful and wise of all God's creation.

Lucifer, along with the other angels at this time, was in perfect harmony with God. There was no rebellion. There was no dissent; there was only one will in the universe, the will of God. Everything was beautiful and harmonious.

The Fall of Lucifer

Everything was harmonious, that is, until one day

when Lucifer decided to rebel against God. The prophet Isaiah reveals the unrighteousness in Lucifer:

> How art thou fallen from heaven, O Lucifer, son of the morning! how art thou cut down to the ground, which didst weaken the nations! For thou hast said in thine heart, I will ascend into heaven, I will exalt my throne above the stars of God: I will sit upon the mount of the congregation, in the sides of the north: I will ascend above the heights of the clouds, I will be like the most High (Isaiah 14:12-14, KJV).

Donald Grey Barnhouse states concerning the fall:

> The next verse in Ezekiel's account gives us the key to the origin of evil in this universe. "Thou wast perfect in thy ways from the day that thou wast created, till iniquity was found in thee" [Ezekiel 28:15]. What this iniquity was is revealed to us in some detail in the prophecy of Isaiah, but there are already interesting indications in our passage that we may not pass by. The fact given here is that iniquity came by what we might term spontaneous generation in the heart of this being in whom such magnificence of power and beauty had been combined and to whom such authority and privilege had been given. Here is the beginning of sin. Iniquity was found in the heart of Lucifer (Donald Grey Barnhouse, *The Invisible War*, Grand Rapids, MI: Zondervan Publishing House, 1965, p. 30).

He then comments on Satan's fall in the Isaiah passage:

> Comparing this passage with the one in Ezekiel, it is evident that the origin of sin in the pride of Satan was soon followed by the outward manifestation of a rebellion of his will against the will of God (ibid., p. 41).

The Emergence of Satan

The sin of Lucifer was rebellion. Five times Lucifer said in his heart, "I will":

- I will ascend into heaven;

- I will exalt my throne above the stars of God;

- I will sit upon the mount of the congregation;

- I will ascend above the heights of the clouds;

- I will be like the Most High.

This rebellion brought the downfall of Lucifer, and when Lucifer fell he was transformed into Satan. By another will coming into the universe, a will which was antagonistic to God, the universe was now in disharmony. When Lucifer rebelled, many of the angels rebelled with him, attempting to overthrow the authority of God. This resulted in Lucifer and his cohorts being banished from both God's presence and His favor.

It needs to be stressed at this point that God did not create the devil. We are often asked, "Why would a good God create the devil?" The answer is, "He didn't." God created Lucifer, the highest ranking of the angels, giving him beauty and intelligence and a position superior to that of every other created thing. He also gave Lucifer a free will to do as he pleased.

Eventually, Lucifer decided to stage a rebellion against God, and it was at this point that he became known as the devil or the adversary. He was not created for that purpose, nor did God desire for Lucifer to act independently of His will. However, Lucifer did rebel and consequently became the enemy of God and His work.

The Creation of the Universe

After the angelic revolt God created the universe as we know it today. We are not told what things were like before God created, so all we can do is speculate. The Bible says, "In the beginning God created the heavens and the earth." (Genesis 1:1). Genesis 1 reveals God's creative efforts. The last and greatest of His creation was man.

The Creation of Man

The Bible makes it clear that man was created by God in His image:

> Then God said, "Let us make man in Our image, according to Our likeness; and let them rule over the fish of the sea and over the birds of the sky and over the cattle and over all the earth, and over every creeping thing that creeps on the earth." And God created man in His own image, in the image of God He created him, male and female He created them (Genesis 1:26,27).

Man was God's crown of creation. He was placed in a perfect environment with everything conceivable going for him. He was in harmony with God, nature, his fellow man and himself.

The Fall of Man

However, Satan was envious of that special relationship God had with man. Genesis 3 gives an account of what transpired when Satan appeared to Eve in the Garden of Eden in the form of a serpent.

> Now the serpent was more crafty than any beast of the field which the LORD God had made. And he said to the woman, "Indeed, has God said, 'You shall not eat from any tree of the garden'?" And the woman said to the serpent, "From the fruit of the trees of the garden we may eat; but from the fruit of the tree which is in the

middle of the garden, God has said, 'You shall not eat from it or touch it, lest you die.'" And the serpent said to the woman, "You surely shall not die! For God knows that in the day you eat from it your eyes will be opened, and you will be like God, knowing good and evil" (Genesis 3:1-5).

The result of the yielding to temptation was a break in that special relationship between God and man.

After the Fall

Since the Garden of Eden episode, God and Satan have been locked into one great cosmic battle, with man as the prize. God is attempting to bring mankind back into a right relationship with Him, while Satan is trying to pull man away from God. Moreover, the Scripture says that unbelieving man is blinded spiritually by Satan in an effort to keep him from coming to Christ.

And even if our gospel is veiled, it is veiled to those who are perishing, in whose case the god of this world has blinded the minds of the unbelieving, that they might not see the light of the gospel of the glory of Christ, who is the image of God (2 Corinthians 4:3,4).

This passage is highly instructive. Satan is called the "god of this world," hiding the gospel of Christ from the minds of the unbelieving people. He will do anything to keep people from knowing God. Besides being called "the god of this world," Satan has been given other titles in Scripture which describe his character and his methods. These include:

(1) *Devil (John 8:44)* is a Greek word meaning "the accuser and slanderer." By calling him this, one is saying that he makes a false accusation against another, one whose aim it is to harm God and man; one who will tell lies of any kind to achieve his end. The popular phrase,

"The devil made me do it," (popularized by Flip Wilson) is really a cop-out. You did it because you made the choice to follow your old, sinful nature. The devil tempts!

(2) *Satan (Matthew 12:26)* is a Hebrew word meaning "the resistor or adversary." By calling him this, one is saying that he reigns over a kingdom of darkness organized in opposition to God. In *The Bible, the Supernatural and the Jews*, McCandlish Phillips says: "Satan is a living creature. He is not corporeal. He is a spiritual being but that does not make him any less real. The fact that he is invisible and powerful greatly serves him in the pursuit of his cause. The idea that Satan is a term for a generalized influence of evil—instead of the name of a specific living personality—is a strictly antibiblical idea ... The less you know about Satan, the better he likes it. Your ignorance of his tactics confers an advantage upon him, but he prefers that you do not even credit his existence."

(3) *Tempter (Matthew 4:3)* describes the enemy's manner of acting. Not content with denouncing before God the faults of men, he seeks to lead them into sin, because he himself is a sinner. For that reason he is called the tempter. He tempts men by promising them, as a reward for disobeying God, delights, or earthly power, or a knowledge like that of God.

(4) *Father of Lies (John 8:44)* describes one of his many tactics. To accomplish his task of tempting men by promising him things, the enemy must lie. Therefore, because he makes great use of lies, he is rightfully given this title. He is not just a liar, he is the father of lies. He hates what God loves and loves what God hates.

(5) *Lord of Death (Hebrews 2:14)*. The enemy has the power of death because he can accuse sinful man. When the Son enters mankind and confronts the enemy with a human righteousness which the enemy cannot accuse, the enemy is destroyed and man is set free.

(6) *Beelzebub (Mark 3:22,23)* ascribes to the enemy a name meaning "lord of the dunghill" or "lord of the

flies." The word is generally believed to be a corruption of Baalzebub, the name of a Philistine god who was considered by the Jews to be very evil (2 Kings 1:2,3).

(7) *Belial (2 Corinthians 6:15)* is a name which originally could be applied to any wicked person. Here it is used as a synonym of the enemy. The word itself means "worthlessness," here used as the embodiment of all "worthlessness," the enemy.

(8) *Evil One (1 John 2:13)* The total effect of all the biblical references is to present the picture of the enemy as one who is the supreme evildoer. For that reason he is given this title.

(9) *Ruler of This World (John 14:30).* Since the world, according to the Bible, is mankind in opposition to God, the enemy as the inspirer and leader of that opposition is given this title, and because his power and might are operative in the present world, he is accorded this title. Similar to this, in 2 Corinthians the enemy is even called "the god of this world." The two titles should give us some idea of the tremendous scope of Satan's power and activity on the earth.

(10) *Prince of the Power of the Air (Ephesians 2:1,2).* The enemy's power, in our age, is operative not only on the earth, but [also] in space (David W. Hoover, *How to Respond to the Occult*, St. Louis, MO: Concordia Pub. House, 1977, pp. 13-14).

In the *Dictionary of Satan* mention is made of various names given to Satan:

Malleus Maleficarum, a fifteenth-century treatise by Heinrich Kramer and Jakob Sprenger, indicates that Satan may be invoked under several names, each with a special etymological significance:

As Asmodeus, he is the Creature of Judgment. As Satan, he becomes the Adversary. As Behemoth, he is the Beast. Diabolus, the Devil, signifies two morsels: the body and the soul, both of which he kills. Demon connotes Cunning over Blood. Belial, Without a Master. Beelzebub, Lord of Flies.

Here are the names by which he is generally known in various languages:

Arabic: Sheitan

Biblical: Asmodeus (or Belial or Apollyon)

Egyptian: Set

Japanese: O Yama

Persian: Dev

Russian: Tchort

Syriac: Beherit

Welsh: Pwcca

(Wade Baskin, *Dictionary of Satan*, NY: Philosophical Library, 1972, p.233).

Satan's Strategy

One of Satan's plans is to convince the world that he does not exist. Denis deRougemont makes the following insightful observation:

> Satan dissembles himself behind his own image. He chooses to don a grotesque appearance which has the sure effect of making him inoffensive in the eyes of educated people. For if the devil is simply the red demon armed with a large trident, or the faun with goatee and the long tail of popular legend, who would still go to the trouble of believing in him, or even of declaring that he does not believe in Him? . . . What appears to be incredible is not the devil, not the angels, but rather the candor and the credulity of the skeptics, and the unpardonable sophism of which they show themselves to be the victims: "The devil *is* a gent with red horns and a long tail: *therefore* I don't believe in the devil." And so the devil has them precisely where he wants them (Denis deRougemont, *The Devil's Share*, pp. 19-21, cited by D. G. Kehl in *Demon Possession*, John Warwick Montgomery, ed., Minneapolis, MN: Bethany Fellowship, 1976, p. 112).

In *The Screwtape Letters*, a fiction work by noted Christian thinker, C. S. Lewis, the demon is recorded instructing his apprentice as follows:

> I wonder you should ask me whether it is essential to keep the patient in ignorance of your own existence. . . . Our policy, for the moment, is to conceal ourselves. Of course, this has not always been so. We are really faced with a cruel dilemma. When the humans disbelieve in our existence, we lose all the pleasing results of direct terrorism, and we make no magicians. On the other hand, when they believe in us, we cannot make them materialists and skeptics. . . . The fact that "devils" are predominantly *comic* figures in the modern imagination will help you. If any faint suspicion of your existence begins to arise in his mind, suggest to him a picture of something in red tights, and persuade him that since he cannot believe in that . . . he therefore cannot believe in you (C. S. Lewis, *The Screwtape Letters*, New York: MacMillan Publishing Co., 1961, pp. 39-40).

There are many false teachers today who encourage people to believe that they do not need to go the way of the cross. The Scriptures warn us against these individuals:

> But false prophets also arose among the people, just as there will also be false teachers among you, who will secretly introduce destructive heresies, even denying the Master who bought them, bringing swift destruction upon themselves (2 Peter 2:1).

Chafer has some apt observations concerning false prophets:

> False teachers usually are sincere and full of humanitarian zeal, but they are unregenerate. This judgment necessarily follows when it is understood that they deny the only ground of redemption. Being unregenerate, it is said of them: "But the natural man

receiveth not the things of the Spirit of God: for they are
foolishness unto him: neither can he know them, because
they are spiritually discerned" (1 Corinthians 2:14). Such
religious leaders may be highly educated and able to
speak with authority on every aspect of human
knowledge, but if they are not born again, their judgment
in spiritual matters is worthless and misleading. All
teachers are to be judged by their attitude toward the
doctrine of the blood redemption of Christ, rather than
by their winsome personalities, or by their sincerity
(Chafer, *Satan*, op. cit., p.78).

Satan will use whatever method he can to keep
people from coming to Christ. If a person has done
many things wrong in his life and feels guilty about
them, Satan will attempt to convince that person he is
not good enough for God, that God would never accept
him. Many people never come to God because they do
not feel God could ever forgive them.

The Bible teaches that anyone may come to Christ
regardless of what he has done and receive forgiveness.
The Scriptures say, "Come to Me, all who are weary
and heavy-laden, and I will give you rest" (Matthew
11:28). Jesus further stated, "All that the Father gives
Me shall come to Me and the one who comes to Me I
will certainly not cast out" (John 6:37). The Bible teaches
that forgiveness is available to all those who will come
to Christ no matter what they have done.

There is another type of person who is also
deceived by Satan but who has the opposite problem.
That person, rather than feeling he is too bad to come to
God, feels that he is too good to need God. Since he has
never done anything in his life which he considers horrible, he does not feel that he needs a Savior. This
person is willing to go before God based upon his own
merit, on the good works he has done in his life, feeling
that God will certainly accept him. However, the Scriptures say, "All have sinned and fall short of the glory of

God" (Romans 3:23); and, "The wages of sin is death, but the free gift of God is eternal life in Christ Jesus our Lord" (Romans 6:23).

Satan's Destiny

Satan is living on borrowed time. God has promised in His Word that Satan and his angels will receive everlasting punishment for the crimes they have committed against God and man.

> Then He will also say to those on His left, "Depart from Me, accursed ones, into the eternal fire which has been prepared for the devil and his angels" (Matthew 25:41).

> And the devil who deceived them was thrown into the lake of fire and brimstone, where the beast and the false prophet are also: and they will be tormented day and night forever and ever (Revelation 20:10).

At that time Satan will be banished once and for all from God's presence without ever again being able to inflict misery on anyone. His eternal separation from God and punishment will be a just end to his inglorious career as the prince of darkness.

What Should Be Our Attitude Toward Satan?

The Scriptures exhort us to take the proper attitude toward Satan in order to deal effectively with his onslaughts. We urge you to observe the following biblical injunctions:

1. Be Aware That He Exists

The Scriptures teach that Satan exists but that he also attempts to hide that fact from the world. "And no wonder, for even Satan disguises himself as an angel of light. Therefore, it is not surprising if his servants also disguise themselves as servants of righteousness, whose end shall be according to their deeds" (2 Corinthians 11:14,15). We already have indicated that one of Satan's schemes is to have people believe that he is a symbolic figure of evil. He would love people to see him as an "angel of light" or even as a funny little man with a red suit and pitchfork rather than as the dangerous, evil, but ultimately doomed adversary of the Lord God and all mankind.

2. Be Aware of His Motives

From the time of his rebellion until his ultimate destruction Satan has wanted to be like the Most High. He wants adoration. He wants allegiance. He wants the service of people who rightly should be serving God. He wants people to believe that it is he who is good and it is God who is bad. However, the worship he desires is not informed worship of a god one knows and has seriously considered.

His deception has people worshipping and serving him without even being aware of what they are doing. He wants to prepare the world for his own world rule through the antichrist immediately before the second coming of Jesus Christ. Lewis Sperry Chafer makes the following insightful observation:

Even fallen humanity would not at first acknowledge Satan as its object of worship and its federal head; and such a condition of society wherein Satan will be received as supreme, as he will be in the person of the first Beast of Revelation 13, must, therefore, be developed by increasing irreverence and lawlessness toward God. Thus it has been necessary for Satan to conceal his person and projects from the very people over whom he is in authority and in whom he is the energizing power. For this reason this class of humanity believes least in his reality, and ignorantly rejects its real leader as being a mythical person. When he is worshiped, it is through some idol as a medium, or through his own impersonation of Jehovah; and when he rules, it is by what seems to be the voice of a king or the voice of the people. However, the appalling irreverence of the world today is the sure preparation for the forthcoming direct manifestation of Satan, as predicted in Daniel 9, 2 Thessalonians 2 and Revelation 13 (Lewis Sperry Chafer, *Satan*, Grand Rapids, MI: Zondervan, 1919, pp. 64-65).

3. Be Aware of His Methods

The Scriptures tell us to be aware of the devices of the devil, for his desire is to destroy the believer.

Be of sober spirit, be on the alert. Your adversary, the devil, prowls about like a roaring lion, seeking someone to devour (1 Peter 5:8).

One of his methods is deception. From the time he deceived Eve in the Garden of Eden until the present day, Satan has been a liar. The Scriptures say:

The one whose coming is in accord with the activity of Satan, with all power and signs and false wonders, and with all the deception of wickedness for those who perish, because they did not receive the love of the truth so as to be saved (2 Thessalonians 2:9,10).

And the great dragon was thrown down, the serpent of old who is called the devil and Satan, who deceives the whole world (Revelation 12:9).

You are of your father, the devil, and you want to do the desires of your father. He was a murderer from the beginning, and does not stand in the truth, because there is no truth in him. Whenever he speaks a lie, he speaks from his own nature; for he is a liar, and the father of lies (John 8:44).

His deception comes in a variety of forms. One of his favorite schemes is to try to make a person feel content without Jesus Christ. If someone does not feel a need for God, he will not turn to God. Therefore, Satan attempts to keep people satisfied just enough that they will not turn to Christ.

In many cases the alcoholic on skid row is much closer to coming to Christ than the successful businessman who thinks he has everything he wants. We often feel that the alcoholic on skid row is exactly where Satan wants him. This is not necessarily so. The alcoholic knows he has a need, knows he has a problem and may be more likely to seek help than the successful businessman who feels content. This subtle type of deception is one of the favorite ploys of the devil.

Another deception used by Satan is counterfeiting. Whatever God has done throughout history, Satan has attempted to counterfeit it. The main counterfeit is religion. Satan loves for people to be religious, to go to church, to think things stand right between themselves and God when just the opposite is true.

If a person believes in some religion without receiving Christ as his Lord and Savior, that person is lost even though he thinks things between him and God are fine. The religious man, trusting in his own works, can be an example of deception by Satan, for God has informed us that to be in a right relationship with Him we must go the way of the cross, the death of Christ for our sins.

We must also acknowledge that apart from Christ we cannot know God. Satan wants people to believe this is not so. Christians are accused of being "narrow-minded" in saying Jesus is the only way one can get to God. The Bible tells us what God thinks of those who try to play down the need for the death of Christ on the cross:

> From that time Jesus began to show His disciples that He must go to Jerusalem, and suffer many things from the elders and chief priests and scribes, and be killed, and be raised up on the third day. And Peter took

Him aside and began to rebuke Him, saying, "God forbid it, Lord! This shall never happen to You." But He turned and said to Peter, "Get behind Me, Satan! You are a stumbling block to Me; for you are not setting your mind on God's interests, but man's " (Matthew 16:21-23).

The Lord was acknowledging the sharp contrast between God's ways and fallen man's ways which are actually identified with Satan's ways. Satan cannot trust in the power of God because he has rejected God. Fallen man has also rejected God (Romans 3:12) and can turn to God only through the mediating sacrifice of Jesus Christ.

Fallen man, often with the approval and help of Satan, has developed a wide variety of religious beliefs in the world as ways to achieve God's favor without submitting to God. Satan is always pleased when people trust in their religiosity rather than Jesus Christ.

4. Be Aware of His Limitations

Satan, the great deceiver, sometimes tries to fool people into thinking he is greater than he actually is. One of the misconceptions that people have about Satan is that he is like God. Nothing could be further from the truth!

God is infinite while Satan is finite or limited. God can be present everywhere at once; Satan cannot. God is all-knowing, able to read our very thoughts; Satan cannot. God is all-powerful; Satan is not. God has the ability to do anything; Satan cannot. However, Satan would like people to believe he has these abilities. Unfortunately, there are too many believers who see Satan behind everything, giving him credit where no credit is due. Basil Jackson makes an appropriate comment:

Today, I believe we are seeing a most unhealthy interest in the area of demonology so that many of our evangelical friends have, in effect, become "demono-philiacs" as a result of their fascination with the occult. They tend to see a demon under every tree and, thus, quite commonly today, we hear of demons of tobacco, alcohol, asthma, and every other condition imaginable. In this connection, it is noteworthy that, by far, the majority of cases of demon possession which are diagnosed in the deliverance ministry today are mental in phenomenology. This is in marked contrast with the only safe records we have of accurately diagnosed cases of demon possession—namely, the Gospels, in which at least half the people possessed had physical problems rather than any psychiatric difficulties (Basil Jackson in *Demon Possession*, edited by John Warwick Montgomery, Minneapolis, MN: Bethany Fellowship, 1976, p. 201).

The Scriptures tell us, "You are from God, little children, and have overcome them; because greater is He who is in you than he who is in the world" (1 John 4:4).

We need to realize that Satan is not all-powerful; he has been defeated by Christ's death on the cross. The power of sin over us is broken. Therefore, we need to respect his power but not fear it. The power of God is greater but the great deceiver would have you doubting that. Therefore, be aware of the limitations of Satan and the unlimited power of God.

The Bible says Christ came into the world to destroy the works of the devil (1 John 3:8). This has now been accomplished. The victory has been won. Satan has been defeated.

Demons

The Bible not only teaches the existence of the devil but also of a great company of his followers known as demons or evil spirits. These demons originally were holy but with the leader, Satan, they fell away from God. Their ultimate end will be eternal damnation when God judges Satan and his host at the Great White Throne judgment (Revelation 20:10-15).

These demons have certain characteristics revealed by the Scripture, including the following:

1. Demons are spirits without bodies.

> For our struggle is not against flesh and blood, but against the rulers, against the powers, against the world forces of this darkness, against the spiritual forces of wickedness in the heavenly places (Ephesians 6:12).

2. Demons were originally in fellowship with God.

> And angels who did not keep their own domain, but abandoned their proper abode, He has kept in eternal bonds under darkness for the judgment of the great day (Jude 6).

3. Demons are numerous.

> For He had been saying to him, "Come out of the man, you unclean spirit!" And He was asking him, "What is your name?" And he said to Him, "My name is Legion; for we are many" (Mark 5:8,9).

4. Demons are organized.

> This man casts out demons only by Beelzebul the ruler of the demons (Matthew 12:24).

5. Demons have supernatural powers.

> For they are spirits of demons, performing signs, which go out to the kings of the whole world, to gather them together for the war of the great day of God, the Almighty (Revelation 16:14)

6. Demons are knowledgeable of God.

> And behold, they cried out saying, "What do we have to do with You, Son of God? Have You come here to torment us before the time?" (Matthew 8:29).

7. Demons are allowed to roam the earth and torment unbelievers.

Now when the unclean spirit goes out of a man, it passes through waterless places, seeking rest, and does not find it. Then it says, "I will return to my house from which I came"; and when it comes, it finds it unoccupied, swept, and put in order. Then it goes, and takes along with it seven other spirits more wicked than itself, and they go in and live there; and the last state of that man becomes worse than the first (Matthew 12:43-45).

8. Demons sometimes can inflict sickness.

And as they were going out, behold, a dumb man, demon possessed, was brought to Him. And after the demon was cast out, the dumb man spoke (Matthew 9:32,33).

9. Demons can possess or control animals.

And He gave them permission. And coming out, the unclean spirits entered the swine; and the herd rushed down the steep bank into the sea, about two thousand of them, and they were drowned in the sea (Mark 5:13).

10. Demons can possess or control human beings.

And also some women who had been healed of evil spirits and sicknesses. Mary who was called Magdalene, from whom seven demons had gone out (Luke 8:2).

11. Demons sometimes can cause mental disorders.

And when He had come out of the boat, immediately a man from the tombs with an unclean spirit met Him, and he had his dwelling among the tombs. And no one was able to bind him anymore, even with a chain ... And constantly night and day, among the tombs and in the mountains, he was crying out and gnashing himself with stones (Mark 5:2,3,5).

12. Demons know that Jesus Christ is God.

And just then there was in their synagogue a man with an unclean spirit; and he cried out, saying, "What do we have to do with You, Jesus of Nazareth? Have You come to destroy us? I know who You are—the Holy One of God" (Mark 1:23,24).

13. Demons tremble before God.

You believe that God is one. You do well; the demons also believe, and shudder (James 2:19).

14. Demons teach false doctrine.

But the Spirit explicitly says that in later times some will fall away from the faith, paying attention to deceitful spirits and doctrines of demons (1 Timothy 4:1).

15. Demons oppose God's people.

For our struggle is not against flesh and blood, but against the rulers, against the powers, against the world forces of this darkness, against the spiritual forces of wickedness in the heavenly places (Ephesians 6:12).

16. Demons attempt to destroy Christ's Kingdom.

Be of sober spirit, be on the alert. Your adversary, the devil, prowls about like a roaring lion, seeking someone to devour (1 Peter 5:8).

17. God takes advantage of the actions of demons to accomplish His divine purposes.

Then God sent an evil spirit between Abimelech and the men of Shechem; and the men of Shechem dealt treacherously with Abimelech (Judges 9:23).

18. God is going to judge demons at the last judgment.

For if God did not spare angels when they sinned, but cast them into hell and committed them to pits of darkness, reserved for judgment . . . (2 Peter 2:4).

Demon Possession

Ever since the release of the motion picture, "The Exorcist," there has been active discussion about the subject of demon possession. Can demon possession, or control of a person's will by a demon, actually occur? What are the signs of a possessed person? Is it really just superstition and ignorance to believe in demon possession? Because of the continual interest in these and other questions, we felt we should address the subject of demon possession.

The Reality of Demon Possession

The evidence from Scripture is *unmistakable* that a human being can be possessed or controlled by a demon or evil spirit (Mark 7:24-30; 9:17-29).

From the New Testament accounts of demon possession, along with other examples, we can chart some of the phenomena that can be observed during a demonic attack.

A. Change of Personality (including intelligence, moral character, demeanor, appearance)

B. Physical Changes

    1. Preternatural strength

    2. Epileptic convulsions; foaming

    3. Catatonic symptoms; falling

    4. Clouding of consciousness; anaesthesia to pain

    5. Changed voice.

C. Mental Changes

    1. Glossolalia; understanding unknown languages [the counterfeit gift as opposed to the biblical gift].

    2. Preternatural knowledge

3. Psychic and occult powers, e.g., clairvoyance, telepathy and prediction

D. Spiritual Changes

1. Reaction to and fear of Christ; blasphemy with regret as in depression

2. Affected by prayer

E. Deliverance possible in the name of Jesus

As this is a diagnosis in retrospect it falls outside the range of pre-exorcism symptoms. (John Richards, *But Deliver Us From Evil: An Introduction to the Demonic Dimension in Pastoral Care,* London: Darton, Longman and Todd, 1974, p. 156).

Does Demon Possession Occur Today?

Granting the fact that demon possession occurred in New Testament times, the natural question arises, "Does it occur today?" After extensive study of demonology and years of observing patients, psychiatrist Paul Meier gives his professional opinion:

I can honestly say that I have never yet seen a single case of demon possession. The main thing I have learned about demon possession is how little we really know about it and how little the Bible says about it.

I have had hundreds of patients who came to see me because they thought they were demon-possessed. Scores of them heard "demon voices" telling them evil things to do. It was at first surprising to me that all of these had dopamine deficiencies in their brains, which were readily correctable with Thorazine or any other major tranquilizer. I discovered that all of the "demons" I was seeing were allergic to Thorazine and that, in nearly every case, a week or two on Thorazine made the "demons" go away and brought the patient closer to his real conflicts. These demons were merely auditory hallucinations. To have self-esteem, these patients were unconsciously amplifying their own unwanted thoughts so loud they seemed like real voices. They felt less guilty when they could convince themselves that these thoughts were coming from an external source ("demons"), rather than from within themselves.

Don't get me wrong, I am a strict Biblicist who believes in the inerrancy of the Scriptures. I believe demons really do exist because the Bible says they do. I believe that there probably are some demon possessed persons in various parts of the world (Danny Korem and Paul Meier, *The Fakers*, Grand Rapids, MI: Baker Book House, 1980, pp. 160-61).

However, there are many others who attest to having witnessed demon possession. Kurt Koch* writes:

I was once invited by Dr. Martin Lloyd-Jones to speak before a group of psychiatrists in London. During the discussion which followed my talk, two psychiatrists stood up and stated quite dogmatically that possession as such did not exist. Immediately after this, however, two other psychiatrists present—they were both Christians—rose to their feet and said that they were not only convinced that possession was a genuine phenomenon, but that they had already come across cases of it within their own practice, one of them seven cases and the other eleven (Kurt Koch, *Demonology, Past and Present*, Grand Rapids, MI: Kregel Publications, 1973, p. 32).

In the nineteenth century there were some striking cases of demon possession recorded in China by missionary John L. Nevius. When Nevius first came to China, he firmly believed that demons belonged to a

---

* In this volume we will refer quite often to the examples of occultic activity documented in the writings of Kurt Koch. The authors do this because Koch is the most well-known writer on the subject of the occult in the evangelical Christian world. However, citing his examples does not necessarily mean that we come to the same conclusions or agree that his examples are clear indications of occultic activity.

bygone era. When he heard firsthand accounts of demon possession, he considered it superstition. However, try as he would, he could not convince the people that what they had heard and seen was a result of their imaginations. Finally, the evidence led him to a change of mind, not only believing the demons existed but also that demon possession was in fact a present reality.

Nevius said this of his experiences:

> I brought with me to China a strong conviction that a belief in demons, and communications with spiritual beings, belongs exclusively to a barbarous and superstitious age, and at present can consist only with mental weakness and want of culture. I indulged Mr. Tu (his Chinese teacher), however, in talking on his favorite topics, because he did so with peculiar fluency and zest, and thus, elements of variety and novelty were utilized in our severe and otherwise monotonous studies. But Mr. Tu's marvelous stories soon lost the charm of novelty. I used my best endeavors, though with little success, to convince him that his views were the combined result of ignorance and imagination. I could not but notice, however, the striking resemblance between some of his statements of alleged facts and the demonology of Scripture. This resemblance I account for only as apparent or accidental (John L. Nevius, *Demon Possession*, Grand Rapids, MI: Kregel Publications, 1968, pp. 9-10).

Nevius then records his many and varied experiences with demon possessed people which eventually led to his change of mind on the matter.

Walter Martin gives a couple of examples of demon possession he has encountered:

> Recently in the San Fernando Valley of California three husky clergymen tried to hold down a 120-pound girl who was possessed with multiple demons. She successfully resisted all three of them for a number of minutes, until she was finally subdued. However, she

was still able to kick one man's shins until they were bloody, demonstrating tremendous supernatural power.

In Newport Beach, California, I encountered a case of demonic possession in which five persons, including myself, were involved. In this case the girl, who was about 5 feet 4 inches tall and weighed 120 pounds, attacked a 180-pound man and with one arm flipped him 5 or 6 feet away. It took four of us, including her husband, to hold her body to a bed while we prayed in the name of Jesus Christ for the exorcism of the demons within her.

During the course of the exorcism we found out that she was possessed because she had worshipped Satan, and because of that worship he had come with his forces and taken control of her. She was a perfect "tare in the wheat field," as Jesus said (Matthew 13:24-30). She had married a Christian, was the daughter of a Christian minister, had taught Sunday school in a Christian church, and had appeared on the surface to be perfectly consistent with Christian theology. But the whole time she was laughing inwardly at the church and at Christ. It was not until after her exorcism that she was delivered and received Jesus Christ as her Lord and Savior. Today she and her husband are on the mission field serving the Lord Jesus Christ.

I have a psychologist friend who was present with me at an exorcism in Newport Beach, California. Before we entered the room he said, "I want you to know I do not believe in demonic possession. This girl is mentally disturbed."

I said, "That may well be. We'll find out very soon."

As we went into the room and closed the door, the girl's supernatural strength was soon revealed. Suddenly from her body a totally foreign voice said quietly, with a smirk on the face (she was unconscious—the psychologist testified to that), "We will outlast you."

The psychologist looked at me and said, "What was that?"

"That is what you don't believe in," I said.

We spent about 3 1/2 hours exorcising what the psychologist didn't believe in!

At the end of the exorcism he was not only a devout believer in the personality of the devil, but in demonic possession and biblical exorcism as well. He now knows that there are other-dimensional beings capable of penetrating this dimension and of controlling human beings! (Walter Martin, *Exorcism: Fact or Fable*, Santa Ana, CA: Vision House Publishers, 1975, pp. 17-18, 21)

In conclusion, although most cases of alleged demon possession turn out to be in reality something quite different, it does not negate the fact that demon possession can and does occur today. However, one should be very careful before he considers an individual demon possessed when the person's problem may be physiological or psychological.

Only a mature Christian, experienced and seasoned by the Lord in counseling and spiritual warfare, should take an active part in diagnosing or treating alleged cases of demon possession. The human body, mind and spirit is so complex and interrelated that it takes spiritual discernment coupled with a great amount of knowledge to deal responsibly with what appears to be demon possession.

If you know someone who appears to be demon possessed and who wants help, you can and should pray for him and direct him to someone who is qualified to help. There is hope for him: God can and will set him free from whatever is binding him, be it demonic, physiological or psychological.

The Scripture exhorts us to "put on the full armor of God, that you may be able to stand firm against the schemes of the devil" (Ephesians 6:11). In order to stand firm, we need to recognize that the devil exists, what his methods and motives are, and the limitations which he has. Knowing this, we can intelligently combat Satan and his attacks by following the principles God has given to us:

> Put on the full armor of God, that you may be able to stand firm against the schemes of the devil. For our struggle is not against flesh and blood, but against the rulers, against the powers, against the world forces of this darkness, against the spiritual forces of wickedness in the heavenly places. Therefore, take up the full armor of God, that you may be able to resist in the evil day, and having done everything, to stand firm. Stand firm therefore, having girded your loins with truth, and having put on the breastplate of righteousness, and having shod your feet with the preparation of the gospel of peace; in addition to all, taking up the shield of faith with which you will be able to extinguish all the flaming missiles of the evil one. And take the helmet of salvation, and the sword of the Spirit, which is the word of God (Ephesians 6:11-17).

9

Satanism

S atanism is a branch of the occult that involves some of the most sinister rituals imaginable. In this chapter we will examine the hosts of hell and the father of lies, Satan himself. The Bible has much to say about the archenemy of God. We are to be aware of his fiery darts (Ephesians 6:16), and to be of sober spirit, resisting him, while we stand firm in the faith (1 Peter 5:8,9).

The Worship of Satan

The worship of Satan has deep historical roots and is expressed in various ways. Black magic, the black mass, facets of the drug culture, blood sacrifice, sexual and physical abuse rituals, all have connections with Satanism.

In *Escape From Witchcraft*, Roberta Blankenship explains what two girls, both Satanists, wrote to her as part of their initiation ritual:

They had to go to a graveyard in the dead of night, walk across a man-sized cross, and denounce any belief in Christ. Afterward, a ritual was performed and the girls had to drink the blood of animals that had been skinned alive (Roberta Blankenship, *Escape From Witchcraft*, Grand Rapids, MI: Zondervan Publishing House, 1972, p. 1).

Lynn Walker comments:

In April, 1973, the battered, mutilated body of a 17-year-old boy, Ross "Mike" Cochran, was found outside Daytona Beach, Florida. An Associated Press story said, "The verdict of police is that Cochran was the victim of devil worshippers: killed in a frenzied sacrificial ritual."

Lynn McMillon, Oklahoma Christian College professor, reports, "One variety of Satanism consists primarily of sex clubs that embellish their orgies with Satanist rituals. Another variety of Satanists are the drug-oriented groups" (Lynn Walker, *Supernatural Power and the Occult*, Austin, TX: Firm Foundation Publishing House, n.d., p. 1).

The South Carolina Medical Association heard Dr. George Bruce explain that thousands of people throughout South Carolina are involved in satanic cults. Bruce explained that the main reason young people get involved in Satan worship is loneliness ("Satanism Dominates 'Thousands' in South Carolina," *The State*, Columbia, South Carolina, Saturday, April 27, 1991, p. 3b).

Sheriff's deputy Lewis Marshall exhorted the medical association that "it's widespread. The hardest job we've got is to let people know it's happening." Marshall explained that "people go into it because they think they'll get power out of it . . . they have ways of getting what they want and also of punishing people."

Deputy Marshall added that "if you want to know

how bad the occult situation is, it runs parallel to drug abuse" (ibid, p. 3b).

The National Crime Prevention Institute has documented 4,500 occult organizations that include ones with military and business ties. They report there is an increasing number of fatalities related to satanic activities ("Satanism: Many Teens Involved," *The Knoxville News-Sentinel*, September 28, 1990, p. A1).

The Black Mass

The black mass is said in honor of the devil at the witches' sabbath. It is practiced by many satanic groups. The ritual reverses the Roman Catholic mass, desecrating the objects used in worship. Oftentimes a nude woman is stretched out upon the altar where the high priest ends the ritual by having sex with her.

Sometimes the participants drink the blood of an animal during the ceremony, along with the eating of human flesh in a mock communion ritual. Human sacrifices, though rare, are not unknown to the black mass.

The black mass contains many other repulsive practices that are unmentionable. It perverts and desecrates the true worship of God and is a blasphemous affront to all believers in Christ.

Clifford Wilson and John Weldon described a black mass as follows:

> Normally, a small group of people sit in front of a table covered with a purple velvet altar cloth, lit with candles. Over the "altar" hangs a cross upside down and a picture of the devil, half-human, half-beast. A high priest stands by the table dressed in bishop's robes. On his person he wears an inverted cross. He throws a larger cross to the floor. "Shehaforash," he shouts. This is probably the most powerful word uttered in satanic worship. According to the Talmud (a book of Jewish civil

and religious laws and ethical lore) it was the secret mystic word spoken by God when He created the world. He then spits upon the cross, with an obscene gesture, and cries, "Hail Satan!" Thus begins the sickening and blasphemous ritual, as the devil worshippers repeat the Lord's prayer backwards and make mockery of the ordinances of the church. One quotation from LaVey's *The Satanic Bible* says, "Blessed are the strong, for they shall possess the earth"; and, "If a man smite you on one cheek, smash him on the other!"

Nudity is commonly found at satanic covens. When a witch is initiated, she is symbolically "sacrificed" to the sun god, and this ceremony takes place while she is lying naked on the altar. The power of the witch is said to be heightened by the mysterious force that is within her own body, and when clothing is worn that power is supposedly obstructed. Their delusion is that they will gain pleasure and enjoyment in this world, especially of a sensual nature and that in a coming age Satan will overcome the Christians' God and return to the heaven from which he was once thrown out. Satan's earthly followers, so the delusion goes, will then share fruits of eternal power with his spirit forces (Clifford Wilson and John Weldon, *Occult Shock and Psychic Forces*, San Diego: Master Books, 1980, p. 10).

The black mass is today's perfect image of the occultism so clearly condemned by the Lord in the Old and New Testaments. It is not possible to serve both Satan and Jesus Christ. Christians should have nothing to do with the black mass or any satanic or witchcraft practices. They are perversions of the true gospel. As perversions, they bring eternal death rather than the eternal life promised by Jesus Christ.

A day will come when even Satan, his demons and those who are bound in the occult will no longer celebrate the black mass, but will be forced to bow to the Lord Jesus Christ:

At the name of Jesus every knee should bow, of those who are in heaven, and on earth, and under the earth, and that every tongue should confess that Jesus Christ is Lord, to the glory of God the Father (Philippians 2:10,11).

Traditional Satanism

Until contemporary times Satanism has had much more secretive associations than at present. In the past, the anti-religious and anti-god aspect was prevalent in all aspects of Satanism. Although this is not true of modern Satanism today, traditional Satanism still is associated with black magic and ritualism.

The worship of a personal and powerful devil is central to traditional Satanism. Those involved reject Christianity, yet choose the Lucifer of Scriptures as their god. *The Occult Sourcebook* comments:

> Traditionally, Satanism has been interpreted as the worship of evil, a religion founded upon the very principles which Christianity rejects. As such, Satanism exists only where Christianity exists, and can be understood only in the context of the Christian world view. Things are, so to speak, reversed—the Christian devil becomes the Satanist's god, Christian virtues become vices, and vices are turned into virtues. Life is interpreted as a constant battle between the powers of light and darkness, and the Satanist fights on the side of darkness, believing that ultimately this will achieve victory (Neville Drury and Gregory Tillett, *The Occult Sourcebook*, London: Routledge & Kegan Paul, Ltd., 1978, p. 149).

Satanic witchcraft is to be found under this category of Satanism, where witches are involved in the darkest side of evil.

The recent onslaught of drugs and sexual perversion associated with the devil can be found here.

In modern times groups have emerged in England and Europe, and particularly in the United States, which, taking advantage of the permissiveness of modern society, have encouraged some publicity. The most famous of these has been the Church of Satan, founded in San Francisco in 1966 by Anton Szandor La Vey, which currently has a membership of many thousands, and has established itself as a church throughout the United States.

Several other groups in America have imitated it, and some groups have also been established as "black witchcraft" covens. The Manson gang, in which a bizarre mixture of Satanism and occultism was practiced, gained a great deal of unfavorable publicity for Satanism in America, but in fact this resulted in a greater public interest in the subject. With more people rejecting the traditional values of morality, the Satanist movement will inevitably have greater appeal (Drury, op. cit., p. 154).

In a chapter on Satanism today in his book, *Those Curious New Cults*, William Petersen comments on the fact that since the mid-1960s Satanism has been making a comeback. He points to the catalyst for the strong upswing as being the box office smash of *Rosemary's Baby*. Of the film he states:

Anton Szandor La Vey, [founder and] self-styled high priest of San Francisco's First Church of Satan, and the author of *The Satanic Bible*, played the role of the devil. Later, he called the film the "best paid commercial of Satanism since the Inquisition." No doubt it was (New Canaan, CT: Keats Publishing, Inc., 1973, p. 75).

Many people are becoming involved in Satanism from all walks of life. They vary in age, occupation and educational background.

Church of Satan

Although the Church of Satan sounds like a contradiction in terms, the emphasis of the organization is on materialism and hedonism. Satan, to followers of this church, is more a symbol than a reality. In this emphasis they depart from other forms of Satanism. They are interested in the carnal and worldly pleasures mankind offers.

La Vey is of Russian, Alsatian and Rumanian descent. His past jobs included working with the circus, playing the organ in nightclubs, and working as a police photographer. All during this time La Vey was studying the occult.

La Vey declares the church is:

A temple of glorious indulgence that would be fun for people. . . . But the main purpose was to gather a group of like-minded individuals together for the use of their combined energies in calling up the dark force in nature that is called Satan (Drury, *Occult Sourcebook*, p. 77).

Of Satanism La Vey believes:

It is a blatantly selfish, brutal religion. It is based on the belief that man is inherently a selfish, violent creature, that life is a Darwinian struggle for survival of the fittest, that the earth will be ruled by those who fight to win (ibid, p. 78).

Emphases of the Church

La Vey is currently the high priest of the church, which espouses any type of sexual activity that satisfies your needs, be it heterosexuality, homosexuality, adultery or faithlessness in marriage. Part of La Vey's philosophy is expressed here:

I don't believe that magic is supernatural, only that it is supernormal. That is, it works for reasons science cannot yet understand. As a shaman or magician, I am concerned with obtaining *recipes*. As a scientist, you seek *formulas*. When I make a soup, I don't care about the chemical reactions between the potatoes and the carrots. I only care about how to get the flavor of the soup I seek. In the same way, when I want to hex someone, I don't care about the scientific mechanisms involved whether they be psychosomatic, psychological, or what-not. My concern is with how to best hex someone. As a magician, my concern is with effectively *doing* the thing, not with the scientist's job of *explaining* it (La Vey 1968) (Marcello Truzzi, "Toward a Sociology of the Occult: Notes on Modern Witchcraft," *Religious Movements in Contemporary America,* Irving I. Zaretsky and Mark P. Leone, eds., Princeton University Press, 1974, p. 631).

Truzzi describes the church here:

Finally, we come to the major satanic society operating in the United States today. This is the international Church of Satan. This group is legally recognized as a church, has a developed hierarchy and bureaucratic structure which defines it as no longer a cult, and claims over 10,000 members around the world. Most of these members are, in fact, merely mail-order and geographically isolated joiners, but there are clearly at least several hundred fully participating and disciplined members in the various Grottos (as their fellowships are called) set up around the world. Grottos are growing up rapidly around this country with about a dozen now in operation.

The church's High Priest and founder, Anton Szandor La Vey . . . has written *The Satanic Bible* (La Vey 1969) which has already reportedly sold over 600,000 copies and is now in its third paperback printing. La Vey also publishes a monthly newsletter for those members who subscribe to it, conducts a newspaper column in which he advises those who write in questions, and he has recently written a book on man-catching for the would-be satanic witch. (Truzzi, p. 632).

There is a list of nine satanic statements to which all members must agree. These are that Satan represents indulgence, vital existence, undefiled wisdom, kindness only to those who deserve it, vengeance, responsibility only to those who are responsible, the animal nature of man, all the "so-called sins," and "the best friend the church has ever had, as he has kept it in business all these years."

The satanic church is strongly materialistic as well as being anti-Christian. Pleasure-seeking could well describe their philosophy of life. What the world has to offer through the devil is taken full advantage of in the Church of Satan.

Teenagers in Satanism

Why do kids, teenagers—or adults, for that matter—become involved in or pursue Satanism? It is not because they are malicious, mad or maniacal. It is because they are needy. They carry a tremendous burden of personal hurts and unfulfilled emotions or desires. They are impressionable. They often are in the middle of family alienation, and they have a low self-esteem. They lack purpose and they have a deep desire to belong; they live with loneliness and a need to be accepted. These young people are strongly influenced by peer pressure, and they crave the power that Satanism promises. All the above needs that can draw a person toward Satanism are enhanced by the Satanists' tremendous appeal to *freedom;* you are free to do whatever you want.

Many young people look to Satanism to have their needs met.

Recognizing the motivation for involvement in satanic worship is key not only to understanding the present phenomena but also in knowing how to cope with it. An article, "Assessment and Intervention With Adolescents Involved in Satanism," states:

A number of primary themes emerge when adolescents express an interest in Satanism. The most common reason for an adolescent's involvement in Satanism appears to be power. Primarily these adolescents feel powerless and wish to develop a sense of personal power. Because adults and peers report fear and disdain of Satanism, these adolescents obtain a sense of power by having an awareness of mysterious things that upset others.

An adolescent's need for rebellion and individualism can be expressed through an involvement in Satanism. Rebellion may be against authority, society, family, or religions. For example, for the individual who wishes to reject Christian values, Satanism may provide an outlet. Many adolescents might become involved in Satanism simply out of curiosity or a desire to understand more about something taboo.

For the adolescent who feels alienated, Satanism might provide a way of belonging to a group. The criteria for membership in satanic groups are not particularly restrictive. To the individual who feels victimized, Satanism might provide a sense of control. For the adolescent who feels disconnected from the culture at large, Satanism might provide a feeling of status through knowledge and awareness they share with others involved in Satanism. . . . Satanism is another form of escapism. Adolescents report that devil worship provides escape from boredom thorough activities in which there is tremendous excitement (Barbara Wheeler, Spence Wood, and Richard Hatch, "Assessment and Intervention with Adolescents Involved in Satanism," *Social Work*, November-December, 1988, p. 548).

Researchers point out that:

Satanic cults commonly focus recruitment efforts on young white males—intelligent underachievers who feel overwhelmed and powerless, who often come from upper middle class homes and who are looking for a thrill.

Kids that have money, that have time on their hands (and) are bored ... ("Satanism: Many Teens Involved," *The Knoxville News-Sentinel*, September 28, 1990, p. A1).

Jacquie Baladis, an ex-cultist, writes about how young people are recruited and brainwashed:

Youth and self-styled Satanists are recruited into the cult by lures promising companionship, excitement or thrills, free sex, free drugs, money, power and recognition. These lures are intensively persuasive to a person from a dysfunctional family whose values conflict with the family or society. Recruitment locations include schools, parks, satanic and non-satanic churches, occult bookstores, bus and train stations, counseling centers, daycare/preschool centers, parties, psychic fairs, science fiction and fantasy conventions, heavy metal concerts, fantasy roleplaying sessions, satanic computer bulletin boards and cult hotlines" (Jerry Johnston, *The Edge of Evil: The Rise of Satanism in North America*, Dallas: Word Publishing, 1989, pp. 98-99).

Conclusion

Whether considering Satan worship, satanic ritualistic abuse, or personal involvement in Satanism, one must remember that the ultimate victory is in Jesus Christ. Satan is a created being and does not possess omnipotent power but rather supernatural power. Remember, "Satan is mighty but God is almighty." When confronting Satanism it is important to know that your authority over spiritual powers is Jesus Christ.

The Bible does two things for us: It assures us of God's power, and it teaches the truth about Satan and all his dominion.

Ephesians 1:18-23 says,

I pray that the eyes of your heart may be enlightened, so that you may know ... what is the surpassing greatness of His power toward us who believe. These are in accordance with the working of the strength of His might which He brought about in Christ, when He raised Him from the dead, and seated Him at His right hand in the heavenly places, far above all rule and authority and power and dominion, and every name that is named, not only in this age, but also in the one to come. And He put all things in subjection under His feet, and gave Him as head over all things to the church, which is His body, the fulness of Him who fills all in all.

Colossians 3:1-3 says,

If then you have been raised up with Christ, keep seeking the things above, where Christ is, seated at the right hand of God. Set your mind on the things above, not on the things that are on earth. For you have died and your life is hidden with Christ in God. When Christ, who is our life, is revealed, then you also will be revealed with Him in glory.

10

Witchcraft

Witchcraft is known as the "Old Religion" and is an ancient practice dating back to biblical times. Witchcraft can be defined as the performance of magic forbidden by God for non-biblical ends. The word *witchcraft* is related to the old English word *wiccian*, "practice of magical arts." Writers of the past have confused Satanism and witchcraft. Even though we see both as branches a diabolical tree, Satanists and witches have a different world view and do not get along well. Satanists practice out-right worship of the devil. Witches do not worship the devil, except for minor fringe groups. Witches are more interested in magical arts and the divinity of nature. Their world view is pantheistic to the degree that they serve gods and goddesses in the divinity of all.

It was during the Middle Ages that witchcraft experienced a great revival. It was an age when everyone believed in the supernatural, and superstition abounded. Roger Hart expressed the climate in the following manner:

> The people of medieval Europe shared a deep belief in the supernatural. The kingdom of darkness, with its devils and evil spirits, was as real and personal as the kingdom of heaven: Magic could be as powerful as prayer.

> The idea of supernatural spirits was universal and ordinary folk everywhere believed in demons, imps, goblins, hobgoblins, poltergeists and other spirits, and in legendary creatures such as vampires, werewolves and unicorns (Roger Hart, *Witchcraft*, New York: G. P. Putnam's Sons, 1971, p. 11).

If someone wanted to become a witch, there was an initiation process. Some of the techniques were simple and some were complicated, but there were usually two requirements. The first requirement was that the would-be witch must join of his or her own free will. The second requirement was that the prospective witch must join paganism and worship divinity in nature.

Witches are usually organized into covens.

> The word "coven" dates from about 1500 and is a variation of the word convent. It means simply an assembly of people, but it came to be applied especially to the organization of the witches' society (Geoffrey Parrinder, *Witchcraft: European and African*, London: Faber and Faber, 1963, p. 39).

Halloween

The day witches celebrate above all others is October 31, which is All Hallows Eve or Halloween. It is believed that on this night Satan and his witches have their greatest power.

The origin of Halloween goes back 2,000 years

before the days of Christianity to a practice of ancient Druids in Britain, France, Germany and the Celtic countries. The celebration honored their god Samhain, lord of the dead. The Celtic people considered November 1st as being the day of death. This was because it was the end of autumn and the beginning of winter for them. The Druids believed that on this particular evening the spirits of the dead returned to their former home to visit the living.

If the living did not provide food for these evil spirits, all types of terrible things would happen to the living. If the evil spirits did not get a treat, then they would trick the living. This ancient practice is still celebrated today where people dress up as the dead, knocking on doors and saying, "Trick or treat," not realizing the origin of that which they are practicing. Nevertheless, it is still considered by witches as the night on which they have their greatest power.

Before the introduction of Christianity to these lands, the celebration of death was not called Halloween. Halloween is a form of the designation "All Hallows Eve," a holy evening instituted by the church to honor all the saints of church history.

Some church historians allow the possibility that All Saints' Eve was designated October 30 to counteract the pagan influences of the celebration of death. While All Hallows Eve began as strictly a Christian holiday, the pagan influences from earlier traditions gradually crept in while the church's influences waned.

Today Halloween is largely a secular holiday, an excuse to get dressed up as somebody else and have a party. However, true witches and followers of witchcraft still preserve the early pagan beliefs and consider Halloween a sacred and deadly powerful time. Having turned their backs on the God of the Bible, they invoke the help of Satan, fallen from God's favor and relegated to darkness.

Witch Hunting

One of the darkest periods in European and American history was the time of the "Great Witch Hunt." Although there had been scattered instances of persecution of the witches as early as the twelfth century, it did not truly get started until the end of the fifteenth century when two significant events occurred.

The first was a papal letter (known as a Bull) issued on December 5, 1484, by Pope Innocent VIII, which instituted the beginning of official action against suspected witches. This Bull received wide circulation and in it power was granted to men who were responsible for punishing witches. These men were known as inquisitors. The Papal Bull contained the following:

Desiring with the most profound anxiety . . . that all heretical depravity should be driven away from the territories of the faithful, we very gladly proclaim and even restate those particular means and methods whereby our Christian endeavor may be fulfilled; since . . . a zeal for and devotion to our Faith may take hold all the more strongly on the hearts of the faithful.

It has recently come to our attention, not without bitter sorrow, that in some parts of northern Germany . . . many persons of the Catholic Faith, have abused themselves with devils, *incubi* and *succubi*, and by their incantations, spells, conjurations, and other accursed superstitions and horrid charms, enormities and offenses, destroy the offspring of women and the young of cattle, blast and eradicate the fruits of the earth, the grapes of the vine and fruits of trees. Nay, men and women, beasts of burden, herd beasts, as well as animals of other kinds; also vineyards, orchards, meadows, pastures, corn, wheat, and other cereals of the earth.

The seventeenth-century view misunderstood witchcraft and confused it with Satanism. The Italian scholar, Guazzo, listed some of the ancient requirements for becoming a witch:

(1) Denial of the Christian Faith: "I deny the Creator of heaven and earth. I deny my baptism, I deny the worship I formerly paid to God. I adhere to the devil and believe only in thee." Trampling the cross, which accompanied this oath, had been from very early times an important part of the ritual.

(2) Rebaptism by the devil with a new name.

(3) Symbolic removal of the baptismal chrism (the consecrated oil mingled with balm).

(4) Denial of godparents and assigning of new sponsors.

(5) Token surrender to the devil of a piece of clothing.

(6) Swearing allegiance to the devil while standing within a magic circle on the ground.

(7) Request of the devil for their name to be written in the Book of Death.

(8) Promise to sacrifice children to the devil, a step which led to the stories of witches murdering children.

(9) Promise to pay annual tribute to the assigned demon. Only black-colored gifts were valid.

(10) Marking with the devil's mark in various parts of the body ... so that the area marked became insensitive. The mark might vary in shape—a rabbit's foot, a toad, or a spider.

(11) Vows of service to the devil: never to adore the sacrament; to smash holy relics; never to use holy water or candles; and to keep silence on their traffic with Satan (Francesco-Maria Guazzo, *Compendium Maleficarum*, 1608, translated by Dr. R. H. Robbins).

How does one describe a witch? The popular view

is that of an ugly old woman riding on a broomstick with a black cat at her side. This conclusion is rooted in the fifteenth-century view of witches.

The second event which helped cause the great witch hunt was the publication of the book called *Malleus Maleficarum* ("Hammer of Witches") in 1486 by Jakob Sprenger and Prior Heinrich Kramer. This publication became a handbook for witch hunters.

The Papal Bull, along with the publication of *Malleus Maleficarum*, led to a witch panic and a 300-year nightmare. People were seeing witches everywhere. Those accused of being witches had little or no defense against their accusers. During this period more than 100,000 people in every European state were executed for supposedly being witches. The brutal methods of the inquisitors is summed up by R. H. Robbins:

(1) The accused was presumed guilty until he had proved his innocence. The Inquisition adopted this pivot of Roman Imperial law; but in matters of belief, vindication was almost impossible.

(2) Suspicion, gossip, or denunciation was sufficient indication of guilt to hail a person before the Inquisition.

(3) To justify the activity of the Inquisition, the offence, whatever it might have been, was correlated with heresy. Thus, the men who killed the bigoted Inquisitor Peter Partyr in 1252 were tried not for murder but for heresy (as opponents of the Inquisition).

(4) Witnesses were not identified. Often their accusations were not made known to the defendant. In 1254 Pope Innocent IV granted accusers anonymity.

(5) Witnesses disallowed in other offenses were encouraged to inform against heretics, convicted perjurers, persons without civil rights, children of tender years, and excommunicates (including condemned heretics). If a hostile witness retracted his evidence, he was prosecuted for perjury, but his testimony was allowed to stand. However, according to the Inquisitor Nicholas Eymeric

(1360), if the retraction was less favorable to the accused, the judged could accept this second testimony.

(6) No witnesses were allowed to testify on behalf of the accused; nor was his previous good reparation as a citizen or Christian taken into account.

(7) The accused was not permitted counsel, since the lawyer would thereby be guilty of defending heresy. (For a short time lawyers had been allowed, especially when inquisitors were sitting on Episcopal courts, and this privilege was resumed in the seventeenth century.) . . .

(9) The judges were encouraged to trick the accused into confession. The Inquisitor Sylvestor Pierias in 1521 told how this could be done.

(10) Although technically allowed only as a last resort, the practice of torture was regularly used, and could be inflicted on any witness. Civil authorities employed torture, but the Inquisition extended and systematized its use. Torture had been sanctioned as a means to discover heresy by Pope Innocent IV in 1257, in Bull *Adextirpanda*, and was confirmed by later popes; it was not abolished until 1816 by Pope Pius VII . . .

(14) Generally no appeal was countenanced (R. H. Robbins, *The Encyclopedia of Witchcraft and Demonology*, New York: Crown Publ., 1959, p. 180).

The Power of Witches

Witches were supposed to have a variety of different powers which kept the people in fear of them. They supposedly could cast spells which would raise storms and magically destroy crops, and they were believed to be able to turn themselves into werewolves and vampires. However, the most feared power thought to be held by the witches was that of the bewitchment, the ability to cause sickness and death.

Roger Hart makes an apt comment:

It can easily be imagined how—in the days when medicine was primitive—various ailments could be mistaken for bewitchment: paralysis, lockjaw, fevers, anemia, sclerosis, epilepsy, hysteria. Such illnesses often displayed symptoms which were extremely frightening to educated and uneducated people alike (Hart, *Witchcraft*, p. 54).

To this list we could add Huntington's Chorea and Tourette's Syndrome. Huntington's Chorea is a disease which does not show up in most of its victims until they are past thirty years of age. This disease causes the victim to behave in a peculiar manner, including involuntary body movements, fits of anger and irritability and a loss of intelligence.

The victim may make strange outbursts of laughter, cry like a baby or talk endlessly. It can easily be seen how a sufferer could be mistaken for being bewitched or being a witch. Huntington's Chorea is also an inherited disease which would convince the superstitious that the bewitchment had been passed to the children.

Tourette's Syndrome is a rare disease which usually begins in childhood. The victim experiences tics—involuntary muscle movements—throughout the body but especially in the face. The sufferer also may kick and stamp his feet. Along with making awful faces, the victim makes involuntary noises which include shouts, grunts and swearing. All of these symptoms are beyond the control of the sufferer but appear to the uneducated as a sign of being a witch, possessed by the devil.

Many today still consider victims of such diseases as demon possessed or oppressed. Research funding into such rare diseases has lagged far behind that of the major prevalent diseases of our day. Such "orphan" diseases (so named because medical and pharmaceutical interests do not want to fund research on obscure diseases whose treatment would not be profitable financially) will probably remain largely uninvestigated until comprehensive research can be funded. However, the little we do know about these diseases leads us to conclude absolutely that one should not be blamed for demonic involvement when he is in reality the victim of a truly physiological aberration.

Salem Witch Trials

America did not escape the great witch hunt. Roger Hart comments on the Salem witch trials:

> Perhaps no single witch hunt has attracted so much popular attention as that which took place at Salem in New England in the year 1692. This American witch hunt was remarkable not merely on account of the large number of people found guilty (Salem was a small community), but also because of the late date at which it took place. No one had been executed for witchcraft in England, for example, since 1684. But above all, the Salem affair has generally been seen as a fascinating microcosm of the whole Western witchcraft delusion (ibid., p. 109).

Although Salem was a relatively small town of about 100 households, the percentage of those tried for being witches was enormous. As historian R. H. Robbins reports:

> All in all, the toll of Salem, a township of a hundred-odd households, was enormous. During the hysteria, almost 150 people were arrested. A search of all the court records would no doubt add to this number. Because of the time taken to convict each prisoner, only thirty-one were tried in 1692, not including Sarah Churchill and Mary Warren, two accusers who briefly recanted. The court of Oyer and Terminer (hear and determine) sentenced to death all thirty-one, of whom six were men. Nineteen were hanged. Of the remaining twelve, two (Sarah Osborne and Anne Foster) died in jail; one (Giles

Cory) was pressed to death; one (Tituba) was held indefinitely in jail without trial. Two (Abigail Faulkner and Elizabeth Proctor) postponed execution by pleading pregnancy and lived long enough to be reprieved. One (Mary Bradbury) escaped from jail after sentencing; and five made confessions which secured reprieves for them (Robbins, ibid., p. 185).

Fourteen years later one of the accusers, Anne Putnam, retracted her charges, stating she and others carried the guilt of innocent blood.

Comment on Witch Hunting

The great witch hunt of the Middle Ages is remarkable for a number of reasons. First, it is remarkable because it lasted some 300 years and took hundreds of thousands of lives. It is also remarkable because it took place during a time of renewed interest in learning.

The people who participated in this craze were not all irrational individuals but were rather some of the most brilliant, educated people of that day. Scientists, philosophers and lawyers were among those who participated in the great witch hunt, showing that superstition knows no educational bounds.

It is also fortunate that much of the persecution came from professing Christians doing it in the name of God. The passages which were used to justify the witch hunt were misread and taken totally out of context. The legal penalties of such Old Testament crimes were part of the then-operating theocracy in Israel.

The Lord God was the King in Israel; He had the right to determine the crimes and punishments against His holy sovereign state. One who participated in witchcraft was aligning himself with Satan, the foe of God. Such an alignment was treason against the government of Israel, a government directed personally by the Lord God.

Even today treason is often punished by death. However, since no nation today is a theocracy, a nation governed directly by God, the penalties instituted then are not applicable. Witchcraft is still evil and is still rebellion against God. It is not treason. Jesus Christ warned that physical death was not the ultimate punishment anyway.

Those who practice witchcraft, displaying their rejection of Jesus Christ, should heed His warning: "And do not fear those who kill the body, but are unable to kill the soul; but rather fear Him who is able to destroy both soul and body in hell" (Matthew 10:28).

Witchcraft Today

Although witch hunting and witch trials no longer occur, the practice of witchcraft continues. The modern witch does not fit the stereotype of the old hag, for many people who are practicing this art are in the mainstream of society. The question is why? Why a renewed interest in this ancient art among both the educated and the ignorant? Daniel Cohen lists a couple of possible reasons:

First, there is the eternal appeal of magic, the promise, however muted, that there are secrets available that will give a person power, money, love, and all those things he or she desires but cannot seem to obtain. Second, witchcraft is a put-down and a revolt against some of the establishment beliefs in organized religion, science, and rational thinking. The historic connection between witchcraft and drugs and sex also has undoubted appeal. Here is a set of beliefs that claim to be part of an extremely ancient religion. Yet this is a religion in which drugs and free sexuality are not condemned, but might be encouraged.

Despite all the publicity and all the witch covens that have been organized, witchcraft still is not taken seriously (Daniel Cohen, *A Natural History of Unnatural Things*, New York: McCall Publishing Company, 1971, pp. 31-32).

Modern witchcraft bears little resemblance to the witchcraft of the Middle Ages or to witchcraft in still primitive, preliterate societies. Modern witchcraft is a relatively recent development (the last 200 years), embraces hundreds of beliefs and practices and has hundreds of thousands of adherents. The one common theme running through modern witchcraft is the practice of and belief in things forbidden by God in the Bible as occultic.

Up until a couple of decades ago, and for previous centuries, there were no admitted witches anywhere. Most people have thought of witchcraft as something that only the superstitious gave any credence to. Witch hunts and broomsticks were filed away together in a little-used corner of the mind.

Today, in a massive spin-off from the culture-wide interest in the occult, this has all changed. Tens of thousands across America—some of them with university degrees—are dabbling in witchcraft, Satanism, voodoo, and other forms of black and white magic. Witches appear openly on television. Every high school is said to have its own witch. In Cleveland you can rent a witch to liven up a party. There are some 80,000 persons practicing white magic in the United States, with 6,000 in Chicago alone.

Some of this is a fad. But unfortunately, much of it isn't. Murder after murder has been linked to the craze, with the murderers openly admitting to police or to reporters that they worshipped Satan. Police, more and more frequently, are finding grim evidence of both animal and human sacrifice (George Vandeman, *Psychic*

Roulette, Nashville, TN: Thomas Nelson, Inc., 1973, pp. 99-100).

Witchcraft is not dead today as can be observed by an article appearing the the *Los Angeles Times* concerning the goddess movement:

Eerie monotones . . . reverberated on the UC Santa Cruz campus. Cheers and whoops went up for the godesses of yore—Isis, Astara, Demeter, Artemis, etc . . . . The event was indicative of a burgeoning spiritual dimension to the women's liberation movement in America . . .

Christine Downing, head of San Diego State University's religious studies department, estimates that many—if not most—spiritually sensitive women in the women's movement are willing to replace the biblical God with a frankly pagan and polytheistic approach.

Witchcraft is aiding the women in their search for roots and rituals—without the connotations of evil usually associated with witchcraft.

A Santa Cruz woman . . . said, "Some of the women think of themselves as witches, but not all."

A brief, unscheduled appearance—met with enthusiastic applause—was made by Z Budapest. A self-described witch . . . the goddess movement knows her more as a leader of the Susan B. Anthony Coven No. 1 in Los Angeles and a charismatic spokeswoman for a feminist brand of Wicca, an ancient women's religion (witchcraft).

The goddess movement, also called the women-spirit movement, apparently considers its first major gathering to have been a conference attended by about 1,200 women at the University of Massachusetts in late 1975 . . .

The ancient Mediterranean world, pagan Europe, Native American and Hindu tradition are all sources for goddess imagery . . .

A religious phenomenon virtually unknown outside feminist circles, "goddess consciousness," will be widely known in three to five years (*Los Angeles Times*, April 10, 1978).

The Bible and Witchcraft

Both the Old and New Testaments make repeated references to the practice of witchcraft and sorcery, and whenever these practices are referred to they are always condemned by God. The Bible condemns all forms of witchcraft, including sorcery, astrology and reading human and animal entrails. The following passages describe the various forms of witchcraft which are condemned by God.

You shall not allow a sorceress to live (Exodus 22:18).

You shall not eat anything with the blood, nor practice divination or soothsaying (Leviticus 19:26).

Do not turn to mediums or spiritists; do not seek them out to be defiled by them. I am the LORD your God (Leviticus 19:31).

Now a man or a woman who is a medium or a spiritist shall surely be put to death. They shall be stoned with stones, their bloodguiltiness is upon them (Leviticus 20:27).

You shall not behave thus toward the LORD your God, for every abominable act which the LORD hates they have done for their gods; for they even burn their sons and daughters in the fire to their gods (Deuteronomy 12:31).

There shall not be found among you anyone who makes his son or his daughter pass through the fire, one who uses divination, one who practices witchcraft, or one who interprets omens, or a sorcerer, or one who casts a spell, or a medium, or a spiritist, or one who calls up the dead ... For those nations, which you shall dispossess, listen to those who practice witchcraft and to diviners, but as for you, the LORD your God has not allowed you to do so (Deuteronomy 18:10,11,14).

For rebellion is as the sin of divination, and insubordination is as iniquity and idolatry. Because you have rejected the word of the LORD, He has also rejected you from being king (1 Samuel 15:23).

And he made his son pass through the fire, practiced witchcraft and used divination, and dealt with mediums and spiritists. He did much evil in the sight of the LORD provoking Him to anger (2 Kings 21:6).

Moreover, Josiah removed the mediums and the spiritists and teraphim and the idols and all abominations that were seen in the land of Judah and in Jerusalem, that he might confirm the words of the law which were written in the book that Hilkiah the priest found in the house of the LORD (2 Kings 23:24).

So Saul died for his trespass which he committed against the LORD, because of the word of the LORD which he did not keep; and also because he asked counsel of a medium, making inquiry of it, and did not inquire of the LORD. Therefore He killed him, and turned the kingdom to David the son of Jesse (1 Chronicles 10:13).

And when they say to you, "Consult the mediums and the spiritists who whisper and mutter," should not a people consult their God? Should they consult the dead on behalf of the living? (Isaiah 8:19).

Then the spirit of the Egyptians will be demoralized within them; and I will confound their strategy, so that they will resort to idols and ghosts of the dead, and to mediums and spiritists (Isaiah 19:3).

Stand fast now in your spells and in your many sorceries with which you have labored from your youth; perhaps you will be able to profit, perhaps you may cause trembling. You are wearied with your many counsels; let now the astrologers, those who prophesy by the stars, those who predict by the new moons, stand up and save you from what will come up upon you (Isaiah 47:12,13).

But as for you, do not listen to your prophets, your diviners, your dreamers, your soothsayers, or your sorcerers, who speak to you, saying, "You shall not serve the king of Babylon." For they prophesy a lie to you, in order to remove you far from your land; and I will drive you out, and you will perish (Jeremiah 27:9,10).

"Then I will draw near to you for judgment; and I will be a swift witness against the sorcerers and against the adulterers and against those who swear falsely, and against those who oppress the wage earner in his wages, the widow and the orphan, and those who turn aside the alien, and do not fear Me," says the LORD of Hosts (Malachi 3:5).

Now the deeds of the flesh are evident, which are: immorality, impurity, sensuality, idolatry, sorcery, enmities, strife, jealousy, outbursts of anger, disputes, dissensions, factions, envying, drunkenness, carousing, and things like these, of which I forewarn you just as I have forewarned you that those who practice such things shall not inherit the kingdom of God (Galatians 5:19-21).

But for the cowardly and unbelieving and abominable and murderers and immoral persons and sorcerers and idolaters and all liars, their part will be in the lake that burns with fire and brimstone, which is the second death (Revelation 21:8).

11

Magic
and
Superstition

Magic

When we speak of magic, we are dealing with a term having a variety of meanings. People use the expression, "It's magic!" when they see something incredible. We also speak of magic being in the air when there is a particularly pleasant mood.

One of the popular uses of the word magic is in the field of show business. Magic shows entertain us when the magician saws someone in half or pulls a rabbit out of his hat. This type of magic is called sleight of hand or, as the French term it, *legerdemain*. It is the art of illusion.

Certain primitive people have a magical view of life with customs and practices based upon sheer superstition. They consider certain phenomena magic because they have not learned the natural explanation of the occurrence (for example, an eclipse of the sun).

However, the magic we are concerned with is none of the above. It is occultic in nature, an attempt to master supernormal forces in order to produce visible effects. This magic is a secretive art, and it is difficult to give a precise definition of all it includes.

Arthur S. Gregor defines magic in the following manner: "Magic is an attempt to gain control over nature by supernatural means. It consists of spells, charms, and other techniques intended to give man what he cannot achieve with his normal human powers" (Arthur S. Gregor, *Witchcraft and Magic*, New York: Charles Scribner's Sons, 1972, p. 1).

Magic, used mainly by witches, is described by Truzzi:

> For some witchcraft practitioners, especially the more orthodox or traditional ones, magic is viewed as a supernatural phenomenon. The character of magic is such that it involves special spiritual agencies (e.g., elementals, demons, etc.) which are outside the natural physical order available for study by empirical science. Thus, for some witches, magical laws are not natural laws, and they can even contradict natural laws. Supernatural agencies and mechanisms are invoked, and these are beyond scientific explanation (Marcello Truzzi, "Toward a Sociology of the Occult: Notes on Modern Witchcraft" in *Religious Movements in Contemporary America*, Irving Zaretsky and Mark Leone, eds., Princeton, NJ: Princeton University Press, 1974, p. 635).

There are different types of magic practiced today. These include:

White Magic

White magic is said to be the use of magical powers and abilities in an unselfish manner for the benefit of others. It is believed a person could be cured of bewitchment by white magic:

> If a child is bewitched, we take the cradle . . . throw it three times through an enchanted hoop, ring or belt, and then a dog throws it; and then shakes the belt over the fire . . . and then throws it down on the ground till a dog or cat goes over it, so that the sickness may leave the sick person and enter the dog or cat (R. Seth, *In the Name of the Devil*, 1969).

A witch in seventeenth-century Scotland described how white magic could be used to cure sickness:

> When we wished to heal any sore, or broken limb, we would say three times:
>
> He put the blood to the blood, till all up stood;
>   The lith to the lith, till all took with;
> Our Lady charmed her darling son,
>   With her tooth and her tongue
> And her ten fingers
>   In the name of the Father, The Son and
>   The Holy Ghost.
>
> And this we say three times stroking the sore, and it becomes whole (Roger Hart, *Witchcraft*, New York: G. P. Putnam's Sons, 1971).

Although white magic was and is used to combat evil, it still comes from an ungodly source and should in no way be practiced.

Black Magic

The opposite of white magic is the familiar black magic which can be defined as the use of magical powers to cause harm to others.

Sympathetic Magic

Sympathetic magic can be defined in the following manner:

Control of a person, animal, object, or event by either of two principles: (1) Like produces like—for example, a drawing of a deer pierced by arrows supposedly would help a tribe's real hunters repeat the scene. (2) Things that were once in contact always retain a magic connection—for example, a man supposedly could be harmed if a lost tooth fell into enemy hands (Daniel Cohen, *Superstition*, Mankato, MN: Creative Education Society, 1971, p. 115).

Sympathetic magic is based on the principle of "like produces like"; that is, things having a resemblance to each other in shape have a magical relationship.

Liturgy of Magic

Often the rituals of magic are similar to the Christian faith. Merrill Unger compares magic liturgy and Christian worship:

A magic ceremony commonly involves the use of four elements—invocation, charm, symbolic action, and a fetish. In the case of white magic, the invocation is addressed to God the Father, God the Son, and God the Holy Spirit. If black magic is involved, the invocation is addressed to Satan and demonic powers. Such invocation is the counterpart of calling upon God through the Lord Jesus Christ. The invocation of black magic is commonly fortified by a pact with Satan in which the person signs himself over to the devil with his own blood.

The charm, which conjures the magic powers into operation, is the counterpart of the Word of God and prayer. The symbolic action, which is multifarious, mimics biblical symbolic action such as forms of prayer or imposition of hands in prayer.

Examples of charms taken from *The Sixth and Seventh Books of Moses* are (1) the transference charm of black magic. Boil the flesh of a swine in the urine of an ailing person, then feed this concoction to a dog. As the dog dies, the ailing person will recover. (2) A healing charm of white magic. Eat, unread, some walnut leaves inscribed with a Bible text. (3) A fertility charm of white magic. Place a woman's hair between two loaves of bread and feed this to cattle while saying a magic verse.

Magical symbolism and fetish. Magic symbolism is intended to give effectiveness to the magic charm and bring about occult transference. Magic symbolism, in turn, is supported by a fetish. This is a magically charmed object which is supposed to carry magical power. Any object, of the most bizarre character, can become a fetish by being magically charmed. The magical effectiveness of the fetish (amulet or talisman) is increased by inscriptions, particularly by magic charm formulas (Merrill Unger, *Demons in the World Today*, Wheaton, IL: Tyndale House Publishers, 1971, pp. 90-91).

Lycanthropy

Lycanthropy is a form of magic which believes human beings under certain conditions can change into animals. The most well-known form of lycanthropy is that a man can change himself either permanently or temporarily into a werewolf. The following sixteenth century Baltic tale gives an example of this transformation:

At Christmas, a crippled boy goes around the country summoning the devil's followers, who are countless, to a general meeting. Whoever stays behind, or goes unwillingly, is beaten by another with an iron whip till the blood flows, and his traces are left in blood.

The human form vanishes, and the whole multitude become werewolves. Many thousands assemble. Foremost goes the leader armed with an iron whip, and the troop follow, firmly convinced in their imagination that they are transformed into wolves. They fall upon herds of cattle and flocks of sheep, but they have no power to slay men. When they come to a river, the leader strikes the water with his scourge, and it divides, leaving a dry path through the oidst, by which the pack go. The transformation lasts twelve days. At the end of this time the wolf skin vanishes, and the human form reappears.

Although lycanthropy is considered mere legend and superstition, there have been modern reports of this phenomena occurring. The following case is cited by John Warwick Montgomery in his book, *Principalities and Powers*, wherein he is quoting from Frederick Kaigh, who alleges his statement to be based on eyewitness testimony:

Now from the distance, out of the bush, came jackal cries, nearer and nearer. The deep growl of the male being answered by the shriller cries of the female.

Suddenly a powerful young man and a splendid young girl, completely naked, leapt over the heads of the onlookers and fell sprawling in the clearing.

They sprang up again instantly and started to dance. My God, how they danced! If the dance of the nyanga (the witch doctor) was horrible, this was revolting. They danced the dance of rutting jackals. As the dance progressed, their imitations became more and more animal, till the horror of it brought the acid of vomit into the throat. Then, in a twinkling, with loathing unbounded, and incredulous amazement, I saw these two *turn into jackals* before my eyes.

The rest of their "act" must be rather imagined than described. Suffice it to say, and I say it with all the authority of long practice of my profession (medicine), no human beings, despite any extensive and potent preparation, could have sustained the continued and repeated sexuality of that horrid mating (Frederick Kaigh, *Witchcraft and Magic of Africa*, London: Richard Lesley, 1947, p. 32).

A summary view of the two main types of magic:

This has led to a common distinction made by occultists between the so-called *black* and *white* magic. In part the view on this issue depends upon the witch's relation to Christianity. For a pure Satanist, the magic he practices is black in that its power supposedly derives from the forces of evil and darkness (though he may regard Christian miracles like transubstantiation to be instances of white magic). But for the witch who has no belief in the Christian's hell or devil, magic derives from special laws in nature. Because of the common public stereotype of the witch as Satanist, however, many non-Christian witches began to speak of themselves as *white witches* and began referring to magic they did as white or beneficial. But this reference to white and black magic was meant to refer to the intentions of the magician in its invocation, not to the character of the magic itself (Truzzi, *Religious Movements*, p. 635).

The Psychic Surgery Illusion

Psychic surgery is a phenomenon which has gained quite a lot of publicity in recent years. The idea behind psychic surgery is that a psychic can perform miraculous operations on individuals by magic without leaving a scar.

The most famous instances of psychic surgery were performed in recent years by a Brazilian named Arigo, known as "the surgeon with the rusty knife." Arigo was a man with little education and absolutely no medical training. His "operations" were performed while he was in a trance.

He claimed that the actual force behind his incredible operations was a spirit that possessed him. This spirit was supposedly that of a German doctor named Aldolph Fritz, who lived during the turn of the century. His methods, however, were anything but that of a qualified physician. Arigo's operations were performed with a rusty knife without using any anaesthetic or antiseptic.

His procedure included the diagnosis of the patient's disease while Arigo was in a trance. His diagnoses wre usually correct. The house in which he performed many of his miracle operations had a sign which read, "Here in this house we are all Catholics." Arigo also would recite the Lord's Prayer before commencing surgery. Obviously, this is not standard operating procedure for surgeons, but the results of this illiterate miner's surgical attempts were amazing.

Kurt Koch lists some of his accomplishments:

I have been to Brazil eight times for various tours. I have also been to Belo Horizonte. In this little town, an incredible surgical miracle was performed by Arigo. Senator Lucio Bittencourt had been holding an election meeting to which Arigo and his friend from Cogonhas had travelled. Bittencourt was suffering from lung cancer and planned to go to the U.S.A. for an operation when the election campaign was over.

The Senator and Arigo were staying at the same hotel. During the night Bittencourt suddenly saw Arigo in his room, with a razor in his hand. He heard Arigo say, "You are in great danger." Then he lost consciousness. When he woke up again, he felt different in himself. He turned the light on and took the jacket off and looked at his chest in the mirror. On his chest was a fine cut. Knowing what he did of Arigo's healing skills, he hurried to Arigo's room and asked him: "Have you operated on me?"

"No, you must have drunk too much."

"I must know exactly what happened," said the Senator. "I will take the next plane and go to see my doctor in Rio."

Bittencourt told the doctor he had had his operation. The specialist took some x-ray pictures and confirmed it. "Yes. You have been operated on according to American surgical methods. We have not yet gotten so far in Brazil." Then the Senator explained what had taken place. This story caused a great sensation in the papers, and brought a flood of visitors to Arigo's clinic.

American doctors, journalists, and camera men went to Arigo's clinic. They carried out all manner of tests, but were unable to discover any deception. Arigo was willing for any test to be carried out. He even allowed his operations to be filmed. An American doctor, Dr. Puharich, even had a lipoma removed. The operation was performed with a rusty knife, without any local anaesthetic or antiseptic materials. Dr. Puharich felt no pain. This operaton was also filmed (Kurt Koch, *Occult ABC*, Grand Rapids, MI: Kregel Publications, 1981, p. 237).

There have been other cases recorded that have not been quite as sensational as Arigo's. Tim Timmons records the following story of a Mexican peasant woman named Carlita. Carlita always operates in a dark room with her eyes closed. Timmons states:

> Carlita's healings are strange! She does not pray over a person asking God to heal them—she actually operates on people with a dull hunting knife! Over the past fifty years, she has performed every kind of operation imaginable—on the heart, the back, the eyes, etc. A medical doctor who had observed Carlita perform many operations was present when I interviewed her. He told of one case where Carlita cut into a person's chest cavity, took the heart out for examination and handed it to him. After she closed the person up, without stitches, she suggested that he go to his hotel room and rest for three days. When the three days were up, he left Mexico City, a healthy man, with no scars from surgery. I asked the doctor what explanation he could give for such an amazing work. He replied, "There is no explanation medically. It's a miracle."

However, not everyone sees these as actual accounts of what transpired. Danny Korem says of the Timmons example,

Carlita was very shrewd in having a physician give credence to her powers. Whether he was duped or participated in the sham is unclear. What is amusing is that she only performs her "surgery" in the dark. Of course, with few conjuring techniques at her disposal, how else could she convince her takers that she removed someone's heart with a dull hunting knife! The statement that the wound healed without scarring in three weeks is also easily explained. A slight cutting of the skin where the operation supposedly took place would heal without a scar. The cut actually gave the "surgery" some validity. The apparent healing again cannot be verified as being imaginary or psychosomatic. Is it not obivous why the psychic surgeons couldn't make the first cut for the American Medical Associaton? (Danny Korem and Paul Meier, *The Fakers*, Grand Rapids, MI: Baker Book House, 1980, pp. 83, 85).

Among psychic investigators there exist differing opinions about the validity of psychic surgery. Kurt Koch comments, "Let us be quite clear about this: Arigo's cures were not a trick or a swindle. They were real operations" (Kurt Koch, *Occult ABC*, p. 238). As already stated, there are others who would vehemently disagree with this stance.

It seems difficult to put all psychic surgery in either category, as being all fake or all authentic. Whatever the case may be, it is certainly not a work of God. In the case of Arigo, he would come under the category of an angel of light. His allusions to Jesus and to the Christian religion are covering the fact that he was an instrument of Satan. The idea of being possessed by the spirit of someone else is contrary to the teaching of Scripture and if Arigo was indeed possessed, it was by a demon, not the spirit of a dead German doctor.

Psychic surgery is not the route anyone should dare take, for the spiritual and physical side effects can be fatal. It is much better to take your physical ailments to the Great Physician.

Superstition

There are many phenomena attributed to the occult which are, in reality, nothing but superstition. Superstition is a belief or practice not based upon fact but upon fear or ignorance of the unknown. Superstition is not confined to a bygone time or to primitive people, for it is with us today. The following are some examples of superstition.

The Number 13

The number 13 is supposed to bring bad luck. This is an ancient superstition still believed by many today. Many builders skip from the twelfth to the fourteenth floor in building construction, fearing the thirteenth floor will bring bad luck. Some feel it is unlucky for thirteen people to dine together since supposedly one of them will die within the year. Friday the 13th allegedly brings bad luck and many people are cautious about the activities they plan. No one knows how this superstition started, as Daniel Cohen comments:

> We do not know how the number 13 got its bad reputation. "Unlucky 13" may have started with the Vikings or other Norsemen. They told the story of a great banquet for 12 guests—all of them gods. The evil god Loki, angry at not being invited, sneaked into the banquet. Now there were 13 guests. One of the gods at the banquet was killed and since that time—the story goes—the number 13 has been considered unlucky.
>
> Some think the belief started with Christianity. At the Last Supper there were 13—Jesus Christ and the 12 apostles. The Last Supper was followed by Christ's crucifixion so that again the number 13 was identified with a dreadful event. It is believed that Christ was crucified on a Friday. This explains why Friday is

regarded by some superstitious people as unlucky, For example, Friday is supposed to be a bad day to start a new job, to begin a voyage, to cut one's nails, or to get married (Daniel Cohen, *A Natural History of Unnatural Things*, New York: McCall Pub. Co., 1971, pp. 5-6).

Breaking a Mirror

Another well-known superstition involved breaking a mirror, which supposedly brings the individual seven years of bad luck. This belief goes back several thousand years to when people believed the image of a person, whether a painting or a reflection, was part of that person, and whatever happened to the image happened to that person.

Prayer for Sneezing

Here's a superstition we all practice without being aware of it. When a person sneezes, we say *gesundheit*, which is German for "good health to you" or we might say, "God bless you." Why no offer of a blessing for a cough? Why only the sneeze?

This goes back thousands of years when people believed one's spirit resided inside his head and a good sneeze might send it away! Since evil spirits were known to be lurking about trying to get into the man's head, his friends would say a prayer to keep the evil spirits away.

Daniel Cohen further illustrates the ancient idea that the spirit could get away from the body:

> When you sneeze, you are supposed to cover your nose with a handkerchief. This is just good sense because a sneeze can spread germs. But why are you supposed to cover your mouth when you yawn? Not to do so is considered very rude, yet yawning spreads few or no germs. This custom, too, started thousands of years ago. At that time, a man was afraid that his spirit might escape though his open mouth or that some evil spirit might

enter. So he blocked his mouth with his hand. In modern times, this ancient belief has been changed. Some parents tell their children to cover their mouths when they yawn, or a fly might get in (ibid., p.12).

Omens

An omen is "an event or object believed to be a sign or token portending or foretelling the evil or beneficent character of a future occurrence" (*The Dictionary of Mysticism*, p. 130).

One medieval writer listed the following as evil omens: "If a hare cross the way at our going forth, or a mouse gnaw our clothes. If they bleed three drops at the nose, the salt falls toward them, a black spot appears in their nails, etc."

Other evil omens include having a black cat cross your path, and walking under a ladder.

Amulets

An amulet is an object of superstition. It can be defined as "a material object on which a charm is written or over which a charm was said, worn on the person to protect the wearer against dangers, disease, to serve as a shield against demons, ghosts, evil magic, and to bring good luck and good fortune" (Frank Gaynor, ed., *Dictionary of Mysticism*, New York: Citadel Press, n.d., p. 10).

In the ancient world, along with many present-day primitive tribes, the carrying of an amulet is a common everyday occurrence. These objects (also called fetishes, talismans, charms) supposedly ward off evil spirits or bring luck to the wearer.

12

Conclusion

The existence of an evil, supernatural realm, led by Satan and supported by his legions of demons, is a reality.

Satan's devices are many, and his methods are as varied as his devices. We as believers never are called to investigate all of these occult phenomena. Preoccupation with Satan's methods is not the best means of approaching our foe, our enemy, the accuser of the brethren. However, this does not mean we are to do nothing.

Rather, as believers, we are exhorted in three major areas. First, we are called to *understand*—understand that Satan has already been defeated. Christ's death and resurrection sealed Satan's fate and destruction. The fact became reality for us when we trusted Christ.

Second, we are called to *know*—know Satan's strategy. Not to know all his methods, but rather his means of operation. This includes his being disguised as an angel of light. Satan's *modus operandi*, aside from a direct assault of lies, also includes the more subtle and often used art of deception. He seeks to lure through the things of the world and the temptations of the flesh. Satan's desire is to replace God's plan with his counterfeit, just as he attempted to do in Garden of Eden.

Third, besides having a good defense of knowing our position in Christ and recognizing Satan's strategy, we must *be on the offensive* in what we do. This means knowing God and making Him known. When we get closer to our Lord and share the gospel with others, it pierces Satan as with a knife—the Lord uses us to advance His Kingdom and bring Satan's domain to ruin. For our mastery over Satan is not in our power, but in God's power and through His plan—sharing the gospel. This is why Jesus said in Luke that we should not rejoice because we have power over demons but because our names are in the book of life (Luke 10:17-20).

Paul clearly states, "For I am not ashamed of the gospel, for it is the power of God for salvation to everyone who believes" (Romans 1:16). Communicating the gospel *is* our goal, even amid all the conflicts that Satan and the world attempt to throw at us. The command to believers is to grow in the gospel and to share it with others.

This is graphically and clearly illustrated in chapter six of Paul's epistle to the Ephesians. The whole point of this chapter is often overlooked, as the emphasis is usually placed on the "armor of God." That is not Paul's point. The whole reason for Paul's emphasis on the armor to stand against the powers of darkness is the need to get the gospel out (Ephesians 6:18-20).

In this section, Ephesians 6:10-20, Paul points out that the true battle stems from the evil forces in the heavenlies, and that his purpose for life is to spread the gospel. His very prayer at the end of the book, which comes in the context of this section on the armor of God, is for him to be able to *make known the gospel*. He places that prayer there by design and not by accident. As Paul saw fit to end his discussion of the forces of darkness in that way, so do we:

Finally, be strong in the Lord, and in the strength of His might. Put on the full armor of God, that you may be able to stand firm against the schemes of the devil. For our struggle is not against flesh and blood, but against the rulers, against the powers, against the world forces of this darkness, against the spiritual forces of wickedness in the heavenly places. Therefore, take up the full armor of God, that you may be able to resist in the evil day, and having done everything, to stand firm. Stand firm therefore, having girded your loins with truth, and having put on the breastplate of righteousness, and having shod your feet with the preparation for the gospel of peace; in addition to all, taking up the shield of faith with which you will be able to extinguish all the flaming missiles of the evil one. And take the helmet of salvation, and the sword of the Spirit, which is the word of God. With all prayer and petition pray at all times in the Spirit, and with this in view, be on the alert with all perseverance and petition for all the saints, and pray on my behalf, that utterance may be given to me in the opening of my mouth, to make known with boldness the mystery of the gospel, for which I am an ambassador in chains; that in proclaiming it I may speak boldly, as I ought to speak (Ephesians 6:10-20).

13

The
Authority
of the
Believer

At the center of the occult, either openly or disguised as an "angel of light," is Satan. Peter exhorts believers concerning our chief foe when he writes: "Be of sober spirit, be on the alert. Your adversary, the devil, prowls about like a roaring lion, seeking someone to devour" (1 Peter 5:8).

Christians often have the tendency to "blame it all on the devil," when in fact it was their own carelessness or fleshly nature which led to the sin or error. It can also be said, however, that even when it is our fleshly nature or the world which draws us from the Lord—and not the devil directly—it is nevertheless true that Satan and his army of demons desire that we be drawn to the world's standards.

Satan is the one who ultimately desires that we pursue the lusts of the flesh, and it is he who sits as the "god of this world" (Ephesians 2:1-10). Though not always directly involved, Satan's prime objective is the defeat of God, and for us that means our defeat.

The authority of the believer spells out the authority a believer has over Satan and his efforts to thwart God's desire for our lives and his attempt to defeat us.

For the rest of your life, one of the most important Scriptural messages you'll ever consider is found here.

As you study the Old Testament, you see that men and women were in a constant struggle with Satan, fighting many spiritual battles. As you study the life of Christ, and Paul, and the other apostles, you see a constant spiritual struggle. Christians today face many spiritual battles.

I'm so glad I learned the authority of the believer before I went to South America. The authority of the believer is a possession that belongs to every true child of God. And it gives so much authority over the enemy that Satan has tried to blind most believers to the authority they have.

During Easter week at Balboa, I first learned of the authority of the believer. About 50,000 high school and college students came down for Easter. With Andre Kole, the illusionist, we packed out a big ballroom several nights in a row—for two or three meetings a night. So many people were coming to our meetings, in fact, that many of the bars were empty. It really irritated some of the people. The second night, one of the men from a night club came over to break up our meeting. They figured if they broke up one of them, that would finish it for us.

As Andre was performing, this guy pulled up with his Dodge Dart all souped up. With a deafening sound, he popped the clutch and went roaring down the street. Everyone inside, of course, turned around and looked out to see the commotion. Finally, Andre got them settled down.

Then the guy went around the block again. As he stopped out front, he revved it up again and roared down the street. By this time everyone was whispering and wondering what was going on. Some stood up, trying to look out the window.

When the guy went back around the block again, I knew that if he repeated his performance one more time, it would break up the meeting. Turning to Gene Huntsman, one of our staff members, I said, "I think Satan is trying to break up this meeting. Let's step out in the doorway and exercise the authority of the believer." So we stepped out and prayed a very simple prayer.

When the guy came back, he started to rev it up again, and as he popped the clutch—pow! The rear end of his car blew all over the street. By that time, we just thanked the Lord and went over and pushed him off the street. As I shared the *Four Spiritual Laws* with him, it reminded me that Jesus said all authority is given to the believer in heaven and in earth. Now, to point out what the authority is, let's look at Luke 10:19: "Behold, I give unto you power to tread on serpents and scorpions, and over all the power of the enemy: and nothing shall by any means hurt you" (KJV).

Two separate Greek words are used for *power* here, but one English translation. The first one should be translated *authority*, not *power*. The Lord is saying, "Behold, I give you authority over the power of the enemy." The Christian does not have *power* over Satan; he has *authority* over Satan. Let me give you an illustration.

I used to live in Argentina. Buenos Aires, the second largest city in the western hemisphere, has six subway lines, one of the longest streets in the world—

almost sixty miles long—and one of the widest streets in the world—twenty-five lanes, almost three blocks wide. One street is called Corrente, which means *current*. It is a solid current of traffic—sometimes considered one of the longest parking lots in the world.

One intersection is so busy, about the only way you can make it across is to confess any unknown sin, make sure you are filled with the Spirit, commit your life to the Lord and dash madly! But one day we approached, and an amazing thing took place.

Out in the center of the intersection was a platform, on which stood a uniformed policeman. About twenty of us waited at the corner to cross. All of a sudden, he blew his whistle and put up his hand. As he lifted his hand, all those cars came to a screeching halt. With all of his personal power he couldn't have stopped one of those cars, but he had something far better; he was invested with the authority of the police department. And the moving cars and the pedestrians recognized that authority. So, first, we see that authority is delegated power.

Second, let's examine the source of this authority. Paul writes:

> And what is the surpassing greatness of His Power toward us who believe. These are in accordance with the working of the strength of His might which He brought about in Christ, when He raised Him from the dead, and seated Him at His right hand in the heavenly places, far above all rule and authority and power and dominion, and every name that is named, not only in this age, but also in the one to come. And He put all things in subjection under His feet, and gave Him as head over all things to the church, which is His Body, the fulness of Him who fills all in all (Ephesians 1:19-23).

When Jesus Christ was raised from the dead, we see the act of the resurrection and the surrounding events as one of the greatest workings of God manifested in the Scriptures. So powerful was the omnipotence of God that the Holy Spirit, through the apostle Paul, used four different words for power.

First, the greatness of his power—in the Greek—is *dunamis*, from which comes the English word *dynamite*. Then comes the word *working—energios*, where energy comes from—a working manifestation or activity. The third word is *strength—kratous*—meaning to *exercise strength*. Then comes *might*, or *esquai*—a great summation of power.

These four words signify that behind the events described in Ephesians 1:19-23 are the greatest workings of God manifested in the Scriptures—even greater than creation. This great unleashing of God's might involved the resurrection, the ascension and the seating of Jesus Christ. "When He had disarmed the rulers and authorities, He made a public display of them, having triumphed over them through Him" (Colossians 2:15). Satan was defeated and disarmed. All of this unleashing of God's might in the resurrection, the ascension and the seating of Jesus Christ was for you and me— that we might gain victory right now over Satan. The source of our authority over Satan is rooted in God and His power.

Third, what are the qualifications you must have to be able to be consistent in exercising the authority of the believer?

First, there must be knowledge, a knowledge of our position in Christ and of Satan's defeat. At the moment of salvation we are elevated to a heavenly placement. We don't have to climb some ladder of faith to get there. We are immediately identified in the eyes of God—and of Satan—with Christ's crucifixion and burial, and we are co-resurrected, co-ascended and co-seated with Jesus Christ at the right hand of the Father, far above all rule and power, authority and dominion and above every name that is named.

The problem is that, though both God and Satan are aware of this, most believers are not. And if you don't understand who you are, you will never exercise that authority which is the birthright of every true believer in Jesus. So the first step is knowledge.

The second qualification is belief. A lot of people really don't comprehend one of the primary aspects of the belief, which is "to live in a accordance with." This is not merely mental assent, but it leads to action. You could say it like this: That which the mind accepts, the will obeys. Otherwise you are not really a true believer. Do we actually believe that we've been co-resurrected, co-ascended, co-seated with Jesus Christ? If we do, our actions will be fervent.

We should wake up each morning and say, "Lord, I accept my position. I acknowledge it to be at the right hand of the Father, and today, through the Holy Spirit, cause it to be a reality to me, that I might experience victory." You talk about space walking! A Christian who is filled with the Holy Spirit and who knows his position with Christ is walking in the heavenlies. I put it this way: Before you can be any earthly good, you have to be heavenly minded. Your mind should be set at the right hand of the Father, knowing who you are.

Often, when I wake up in the morning, while my eyes are still closed, I go over my position in Christ, thanking the Holy Spirit for indwelling me, etc. But every morning, I acknowledge my position in Christ. I don't have to drum it up—I ask the Holy Spirit to make my position real in my experience.

The third qualification is humility. While belief introduced us to our place of throne power at the right hand of the Father, only humility will ensure that we can exercise that power continuously. Let me tell you, ever since Mr. and Mrs. Adam occupied the garden of Eden, man has needed to be reminded of his limitations. Even regenerated man thinks he can live without seriously considering his total dependence upon God.

Yet, humility to me is not going around saying, "I'm nothing, I'm nothing. I'm just the dirt under the toenail. When I get to heaven all I want is that little old dinky cabin, that's enough for me." That's an insult to Christ. It's not humility—it's pride. Humility is knowing who you are and knowing who made you who you are and giving Him the glory for it. Sometimes, when I hear a person claim he's nothing, I say, "Look sir, I don't know about you, but I'm someone." I *am* someone. On December 19, 1959, at 9:30 at night, Jesus Christ made me a child of God, and I'm sure not going to say I'm nothing. Maybe I'm not all I should be, but I am more that I used to be, and God's not finished with me yet. I know He has made me, and I won't insult what God has made.

The next qualification, the fourth one, is boldness. Humility allows the greatest boldness. True boldness is faith in full manifestation. When God has spoken and you hold back, that is not faith, it is sin. We need men and women who have set their minds at the right hand of the Father and who fear no one but God. True boldness comes from realizing your position in Jesus Christ and being filled with the Holy Spirit.

The fifth and final qualification is awareness, a realization that being at the right hand of the Father also puts you in the place of the most intense spiritual conflict. The moment your eyes are open to the fact that you are in that place, that you have been co-resurrected, co-ascended and co-seated with Christ, Satan will do everything he possibly can to wipe you out, to discourage you. You become a marked individual. The last thing Satan wants is a Spirit-filled believer who knows his throne rights. Satan will start working in your life to cause you not to study or appropriate the following principles which show you how to defeat him.

Going through all the above was necessary to lay a foundation on which you can exercise the authority of the believer. Here is how I do it. Remember, authority is delegated power. Usually I speak right out loud and address Satan directly, "Satan, in the name of the Lord Jesus Christ . . . " I always use this point first because those three names—Lord, Jesus and Christ—describe His crucifixion, burial, resurrection and seating, and His victory over Satan. "Satan, in the name of the Lord Jesus Christ and His shed blood on the cross, I command you to stop your activities in this area." Or, "Satan, in the name of the Lord Jesus Christ and His shed blood on the cross, I acknowledge that the victory is Jesus' and all honor and glory in this situation go to Him." I speak to Satan in various ways, but I always use those beginning phrases because they remind him that he is already defeated.

Next, I realized there is nothing I can do. I have no power over Satan, I only have authority. And the more I learn of the power behind me, the force behind me, the greater boldness I have in exercising the authority of the believer.

Once the authority of the believer is exercised, though, we must be patient. Never have I exercised that authority that I did not see Satan defeated, but I have had to learn to wait.

Some time ago, for example, I was to speak in the university in South America. Because of the university's Marxist leanings, I was the first American to speak there in four years and it was a tense situation. Big photographs of me had been posted all over campus and the Communist students, trying to influence the other students to stay away from the meeting, had painted "CIA Agent" in red letters across the posters. I thought CIA meant "Christ in Action." Anyway, it backfired. Most of the students had never seen a CIA agent, so they come to the meeting to see what one looked like, and the room was packed. However, as is often the case when someone speaks in that part of the world, professional Marxist agitators had also come, and their intent was to disrupt the meeting.

When I go to another country I like to speak as well as possible in the language of that country. So I pointed out to the audience that I was learning their language and that night I would be lecturing in it. Well, I started, and, oh, it was horrible! My back was against the wall—the chairs were about five inches from me. And one after another these agitators would jump up and throw accusations at me, call me "a filthy pig," etc., and hurl words at me that I didn't even know. Right in front of the audience they twisted me around their little fingers. I couldn't answer them; I didn't even know what they were saying. I felt so sorry for the Christians who were there because they had looked forward so eagerly to my coming to the campus and to seeing people come to Christ.

After forty-five minutes of this heckling, I just felt like crying. I literally wanted to crawl under the carpet. My wife asked me one time, "Honey, what's the darkest situation you've ever been in?" And I said, "It was that one."

By this time I was ready to give up. Every time I even mentioned the name of Jesus they laughed. I had exercised the authority of the believer, and now I thought, "God, why aren't You doing something? Why isn't Satan defeated?" Well, I wasn't walking by faith. You see, God works when it brings the greatest honor and glory to His name, not to ours.

Finally, God started to work. The secretary of the

Revolutionary Student Movement stood up, and everyone else became silent. I figured she must be someone important.

She was quite an outspoken woman, and I didn't know what to expect. But this is what she said. "Mr. McDowell, if I become a Christian tonight, will God give me the love for people that you have shown for us?"

Well, I don't have to tell you what happened. It broke just about everyone's heart who was there, and we had fifty-eight decisions for Christ.

I've learned to exercise the authority of the believer and then to walk by faith and to wait. Sometimes I have had to wait six months or a year, but in the long run, when I look back on a situation and see how God has been glorified, it is beautiful.

And I never repeat the exercise of the authority of the believer in a given situation. Satan only needs one warning. God will take care of it from there. Jesus said, "All authority has been give to me in heaven and earth. Go therefore, and make disciples of all nations."

Appendix A

Ministry Referrals

The following ministries deal with the occult and can be contacted for further information:

Answers In Action, P. O. Box 2067, Costa Mesa, CA 92626

C.A.R.I.S., P. O. Box 1659, Milwaukee, WI 53201

Christian Research Institute, P. O. Box 500, San Juan Capistrano, CA 92693

Jude 3 Missions, P. O. Box 1901, Orange, CA 92668

Reel to Real Ministries, P. O. Box 4145, Gainsville, FL 32613 (specific research on the occult and Satanism in rock and rap music)

Spiritual Counterfeits Project, P. O. Box 2418, Berkeley, CA 94702

Appendix B

Would You Like to Know God Personally?

H ere are four principles that clearly explain the gospel message and the truth of what God has done through His Son Jesus Christ for each and every human being. We've had great success sharing these principles with those who are involved in the occult, and we've led many to the love of the one true God. It is our prayer that you'll find them helpful as you witness.

1. God loves you, and created you to know Him personally.

While the Bible is filled with assurances of God's love, perhaps the most telling verse is John 3:16:

For God so loved the world, that He gave His only begotten Son, that whoever believes in Him should not perish, but have eternal life.

God not only loves each of us enough to give His only Son for us; He desires that we come to know Him personally:

> Now this is eternal life; that they may know you, the only true God, and Jesus Christ, whom you have sent (John 17:3, NIV).

What, then, prevents us from knowing God personally?

2. Men and women are sinful and separated from God, so we cannot know Him personally or experience His love.

We were all created to have fellowship with God; but, because of mankind's stubborn self-will, we chose to go our own independent way and fellowship with God was broken. This self-will, characterized by an attitude of active rebellion or passive indifference, is evidence of what the Bible calls sin.

> For all have sinned and fall short of the glory of God (Romans 3:23, NIV).

The Bible also tells us that "the wages of sin is death" (Romans 6:23, NIV), or spiritual separation from God. When we are in this state, a great gulf separates us from God, because He cannot tolerate sin. People often try to bridge the gulf by doing good works or devoting themselves to religious or New Age practices, but the Bible clearly teaches that there is only one way to bridge this gulf . . .

3. Jesus Christ is God's ONLY provision for our sin. Through Him alone we can know God personally and experience His love.

God's Word records three important facts to verify

this principle: (1) Jesus Christ died in our place; (2) He rose from the dead; and (3) He is our only way to God:

> But God demonstrates His own love toward us, in that while we were yet sinners, Christ died for us (Romans 5:8).

> Christ died for our sins . . . He was buried . . . He was raised on the third day, according to the Scriptures . . . He appeared to Peter, then to the twelve. After that He appeared to more than five hundred . . . (1 Corinthians 15:3-6).

> Jesus said to him, "I am the way, and the truth, and the life; no one comes to the Father, but through Me" (John 14:6).

Thus, God has taken the loving initiative to bridge the gulf which separates us from Him by sending His Son, Jesus Christ, to die on the cross in our place to pay the penalty for our sin. But it is not enough just to know these truths . . .

4. We must individually receive Jesus Christ as Savior and Lord; then we can know God personally and experience His love.

John 1:12 records:

> But as many as received Him, to them He gave the right to become children of God, even to those who believe in His name.

What does it mean to "receive Christ"? The Scriptures tell us that we receive Christ through faith—not through "good works" or religious endeavors:

> For by grace you have been saved through faith; and

that not of yourselves, it is the gift of God; not as a result of works, that no one should boast (Ephesians 2:8,9).

We're also told that receiving Christ means to personally invite Him into our lives:

(Christ is speaking): Behold, I stand at the door and knock; if anyone hears My voice and opens the door, I will come in to him (Revelation 3:20).

Thus, receiving Christ involves turning to God from self and trusting Christ to come into our lives to forgive our sins and to make us the kind of people He wants us to be.

If you are not sure whether you have ever committed your life to Jesus Christ, we encourage you to do so—today! Here is a suggested prayer which has helped millions of men and women around the world express faith in Him and invite Him into their lives:

Lord Jesus, I want to know You personally. Thank You for dying on the cross for my sins. I open the door of my life and receive You as my Savior and Lord. Thank You for forgiving my sins and giving me eternal life. Take control of the throne of my life. Make me the kind of person You want me to be.

If this prayer expresses the desire of your heart, why not pray it now? If you mean it sincerely, Jesus Christ will come into your life, just as He promised in Revelation 3:20. He keeps His promises! And there is another key promise to write indelibly in your mind:

And the witness is this, that God has given us eternal life, and this life is in His Son. He who has the Son has the life; he who does not have the Son of God does not have the life. These things I have written to you who believe in the name of the Son of God, in order that you may **know** that you have eternal life (1 John 5:11-13).

That's right—the man or woman who personally receives Christ as Savior and Lord is assured of everlasting life with Him in heaven. So, in summary, when you received Christ by faith, as an act of your will, many wonderful things happened including the following:

1. Christ came into your life (Revelation 3:20; Colossians 1:27).

2. Your sins were forgiven (Colossians 1:14).

3. You became a child of God (John 1:12).

4. You received eternal life (John 5:24).

5. You began the great adventure for which God created you (John 10:10; 1 Thessalonians 5:18).

If you have received Jesus Christ as your Savior and Lord, we'd like to welcome you to the family of God! We heartily encourage you to attend and participate in a church where the Lord Jesus Christ is glorified, where the Holy Bible is honored and taught, and where believers love, encourage, and pray for one another. Study God's Word regularly and apply it to your daily life. Share His love with your family, friends, and neighbors.

The truth that the occult claims to have can only be found in the Lord Jesus Christ. We rejoice with you that you've made this discovery of truth in your own life.

These four principles are adapted from *Would You Like to Know God Personally?* (San Bernardino, CA: Here's Life Publishers, 1987). Used by permission.

Homeopathy pg. 105-109